Shop Drawings of Shaker Furniture and Woodenware

Volume 3

Measured Drawings

by Ejner Handberg

Berkshire Traveller Press

An Imprint of BERKSHIRE HOUSE, Publishers

Stockbridge, Massachusetts

ACKNOWLEDGMENTS

This third volume of *Shop Drawings of Shaker Furniture and Woodenware* includes more large pieces of Shaker Case Furniture than in Volumes 1 and 2.

I wish to express my sincere thanks to the following museums and galleries for permission to make measured drawings of Shaker furniture: The Boston Museum of Fine Arts, Boston, Mass.; The Shaker Museum, Old Chatham, N.Y.; The Hancock Shaker Village, Hancock, Mass.; Shakertown at Pleasant Hill, Harrodsburg, Ky.; Shakertown at South Union, Ky.; Canterbury Shaker Museum, East Canterbury, N.H.; Green Willow Farm Gallery, Chatham, N.Y. Also special thanks are due Mrs. Edward Deming Andrews for the help and information given me and to private collectors for allowing me to examine and make drawings of Shaker pieces in their collections.

I hope that these drawings will be helpful to collectors and craftsmen alike.

E.H.
1977

Photographs by Ejner Handberg

SHOP DRAWINGS OF SHAKER FURNITURE AND WOODENWARE, VOL. 3
Copyright ©1977, 1991 by Ejner P. Handberg.

ISBN 0-936399-19-8; previously ISBN 0-912944-45-5
Library of Congress No. 73-83797

Printed in the United States of America

14th Printing

ABOUT THE AUTHOR

This is the third book in the series on Shaker furniture and artifacts by Ejner Handberg.

Mr. Handberg was a skilled cabinetmaker with more than fifty years' experience who first became interested in Shaker furniture and design when people brought the valuable Shaker pieces to him to repair or restore. Born in Denmark, he came to the U.S. at 17 years of age and learned his craft from 19th-century cabinetmakers who insisted upon precision and accuracy.

Volume I and II in this series on Shaker Furniture and Woodenware each contain meticulous drawings of many different types of Shaker chairs, boxes, tables, stools, knobs, candlesticks, trays, benches and similar pieces.

Volume III includes many larger items, such as rocking chairs, tables, school desks, sewing stands, cupboards, a storage bench, a clock case, an upright desk, a dining table, a lantern, pine cupboards, a settee, and counters.

In these three books, Mr. Handberg exercised extreme care to perfect measured drawings of these original Shaker pieces for the purpose of reproducing them in his own shop. Each drawing in every book is unique because it is carefully measured from an original Shaker piece. He emulated the reverence that these unusual people had for wood and the purely functional purpose in furniture.

The informed amateur worker in wood, as well as the professional cabinetmaker and the enthusiastic collector will find Mr. Handberg's books a valuable addition to the perpetuation of Shaker qualities.

PREFACE

This is not an attempt to write a book about the Shakers and their furniture. There are already excellent books which serve that purpose. I refer especially to those by Dr. and Mrs. Edward Deming Andrews. Rather, this is a collection of measured drawings made to scale and with dimensions and details accurately copied from Shaker pieces which have been in my shop for restoration or reproduction. These drawings and patterns have been accumulated over a period of many years of interest in the woodwork of the New England and New York State Shakers.

E.H.

1977

FOREWORD

Ejner (pronounced Eye' ner) Handberg was born in Viborg, Denmark, in 1902. When he was seventeen, he moved to New York. For most of his life, Ejner was a builder in Berkshire County, Massachusetts.

His interest in working with wood began in boyhood on his way to school, when every day he passed a shop where a man worked at a lathe in the window. One of his first jobs as a young man was building lead-lined shipping crates for a Danish firm in New York that made blueprint paper. As a builder, he was perhaps best known for his addition to the handsome old Congregational Church in Stockbridge, and for the studio in the same town that he built for Norman Rockwell in a carriage shed that had been stripped down to the frame.

Building was a way to make a living, according to his wife Elsie, but Ejner's real love was cabinetwork. In 1960, the Handbergs built the Pinewood Shop on Route 102 in Lee, not far from Stockbridge, with a large workshop for Ejner and a gift shop, where Elsie, who was skilled in sewing, offered things that they made.

Ejner's involvement with Shaker furniture began with a chance meeting with Faith and Edward Deming Andrews, noted authorities on the Shakers and residents of nearby Pittsfield. In search of a good cabinetmaker to repair Shaker pieces and a good seamstress for a sewing project, Dr. and Mrs. Andrews had been told of a husband and wife in Lee with those talents. They showed up at the Handberg shop, and in spite of the fact that it was not the Handbergs for whom the Andrewses had been looking, the two couples hit it off.

The visit was the beginning of a friendship as well as a working relationship. The Andrewses often stopped by on Saturdays for tea and-something Faith had baked, frequently bringing Shaker furniture items for repair. In the course of his work, and to satisfy his own interest, Ejner began to make lifesize measured drawings of the pieces he handled, scouting the local dump for large refrigerator and stove cartons to get cardboard big enough for his work. In time, a thick stack of drawings accumulated.

Dr. and Mrs. Andrews, who appreciated the kind of understanding that results from the careful examination necessary to produce accurate drawings, urged the Handbergs to publish Ejner's work. The first book, published in 1973, by Berkshire Traveller Press was a family effort. Ejner redrew the pieces to a smaller scale, Elsie did the writing, and their daughter Anne typed the manuscript. Ejner and Elsie collaborated on the four Shaker books that followed, and a last book on measured drawings of 18th-century American furniture in 1983. Ejner died two years later.

Ejner Handberg's books have sold more widely than perhaps any other books on the Shakers. A large part of their appeal is their practical nature and their utter lack of pretense -- both, characteristics of Shaker work as well. Did Ejner appreciate the visual kinship between Shaker furniture and contemporary Danish design? No, says Elsie Handberg, adding that her husband didn't even like Danish Modern. Did the Handbergs develop a friendship with the few Shakers who remained at Hancock, Massachusetts, or New Lebanon, New York, as the Andrewses had? No, they didn't; Shaker furniture appealed to them in a way that the Shakers' way of life did not.

Today, Ejner Handberg's straightforward look at Shaker work continues to draw admirers into the Shaker sphere. I am grateful to Elsie Handberg and Anne Handberg Oppermann for insights and reminiscences.

June Sprigg, Curator
Hancock Shaker Village
Pittsfield, Massachusetts
1991

CONTENTS

NOTES TO THE CRAFTSMAN OR COLLECTOR

The Shakers used local woods for their furniture mainly from their own land, and all lumber was carefully dried. In the Northeast, large case furniture such as cupboards, chests of drawers, blanket chests, wood boxes and washstands were nearly always made of Eastern white pine. Tables, stands and desks (both writing desks and sewing desks) were often constructed of mixed woods such as cherry, maple, butternut and others. Maple, birch and cherry were used in all pieces requiring strength and withstanding wear such as chairs and stools, of which there were many kinds. Hickory and ash were used for parts which were to be bent. Sometimes candlestands, work stands and sewing stands were made of cherry, maple or birch with a pine top. One feature in Shaker furniture and woodenware was the use of quarter-sawn, edge-grained pine which is less apt to cup or warp than flat-grained boards.

Occasionally pieces can be seen made entirely of walnut, chestnut, butternut and also, but not so often, one can find a small stand, table or chair made of birds-eye maple, curly maple or tiger maple. It is not unusual to see a piece of Shaker furniture where more than one kind of wood was used, as for example, the table legs of cherry, the frame or skirt of maple and the top of pine.

The making of freestanding or movable pieces for use in the early workshops and dwelling houses probably preceded the cupboards and drawers which were permanently built into the walls of many buildings. These were usually six to eight feet high and in no particular pattern, sometimes numbering a hundred or more cupboards and drawers on one wall.

Their furniture was not designed and made for show. There were no fancy turnings or mouldings; everything was designed and made for a purpose, for the Shakers had only utility in mind. There is a Shaker saying "that which has the highest use possesses the greatest beauty."

The eventual result was an original and very simple but beautiful style, that was all their own. From the beginning they continued to improve their methods looking only for strength and lightness. Yet there was always a freedom to make new designs and, because of this, it is seldom possible to find, for example, two trestle tables or two sewing desks which are alike.

An Elder from New Lebanon once said "We find out by trial what is best and when we have found a good thing we stick to it."

It is perhaps fair to say that their furniture was the forerunner of our present day functional furniture.

On all candlestands, sewing stands or other stands with a pedestal, the legs are dovetailed to the shaft and the grain should run as nearly parallel to the general direction of the leg as possible; a thin metal plate should be fastened to the underside of the shaft and extend about three quarters of an inch along the base of each leg, with a screw or nail put in the leg to keep them from spreading.

The first furniture made by the Shakers was usually given a coat of paint, such as dark red for the furniture in the workshops. Later the paint was thinned or stain was used, often so thin that the grain of the wood was visible. Also used was a light umber or raw sienna stain giving the furniture a light brown color. Some pieces were left with a natural finish, then a final coat of oil or varnish was applied. Beds were painted green, almost bottle green, but shades varied.

So far I have only mentioned furniture, but under the heading of "Woodenware," the Shakers made hundreds of very beautiful and interesting items such as oval boxes, sewing boxes, carriers, trays, dippers, cups, scoops, candle and cutlery boxes, berry boxes and hundreds of specially designed tools and gadgets for the use of both the Sisters and Brethren in their workshops and kitchens. Some of the woodenware and other items were made to sell from their salesrooms to the outside world such as the beautiful oval boxes and sewing boxes. The oval boxes and carriers were usually made of maple. The bottoms and covers were fitted with quarter-sawn edge-grained pine. First the "fingers" or "lappers" are cut on the maple bands, then steamed and wrapped around an oval form, then the fingers are fastened with small copper or iron rivets (tacks) after they are dry and sanded. The pine disks are fitted into the bottom and cover and fastened with small square copper or iron brads.

When making a reproduction, I believe you must copy exactly every detail of the original, and use the same kind of wood and finish, because if you change such things as dimensions or profiles of mouldings, or cut-outs, then you are not making a true reproduction, but only a Shaker type piece of furniture.

Although I firmly believe than *no one* can make an "Antique" you should always mark your copy somewhere on the back or the bottom with your name and date in a way that it can not be erased. Please do not make any attempt to give it distress marks.

All this is not to say that it is wrong to make changes or design your own, but you are then making only a Shaker type piece of furniture. As a matter of fact, I have made for myself a secretary or what the Shakers properly would have called an upright desk, which follows very closely the design of two original Shaker pieces. The bottom section is a chest of drawers and the top section is a fall-front desk with place for papers and books, two small drawers, and above are two shelves with two doors (see pages number 76, 77). I never try to call it anything but a Shaker type of desk.

Whether you prefer to copy an original Shaker piece or design your own, I think it most important to carefully select the right kind of wood for the different projects, and be sure it is properly dried before using it. Another important rule is to follow good Shaker design and proportions. This applies to any kind of furniture, because without that, neither good materials nor the best of workmanship will produce good results. Finally you should never start anything before having made a detailed and measured drawing of the piece of furniture or work in mind.

I hope that these drawings will be helpful to craftsmen and collectors alike.

E.H.

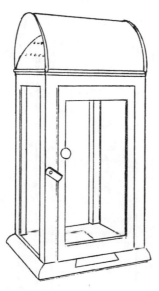

"ALL BEAUTY THAT HAS NOT
A FOUNDATION IN USE SOON
GROWS DISTASTEFUL AND NEEDS
CONTINUAL REPLACEMENT"

PIE-SAFE
WITH PIERCED TIN PANELS
SOUTH UNION, KENTUCKY

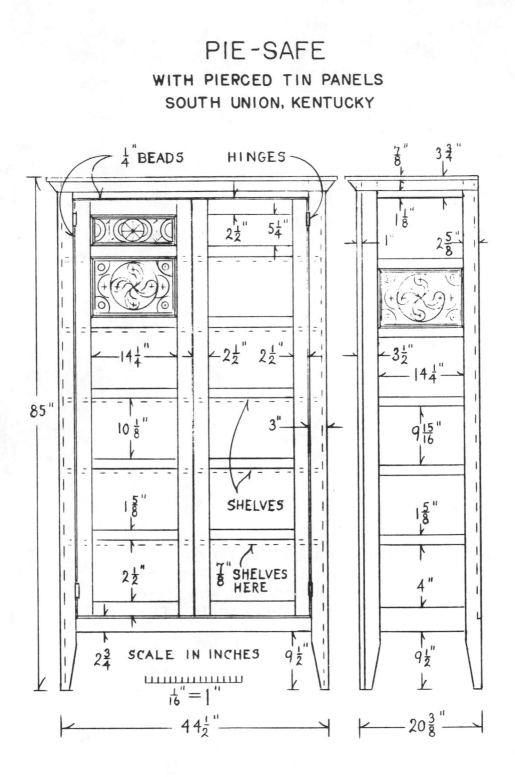

$\frac{1}{4}$" BEADS HINGES

$2\frac{1}{2}$" $5\frac{1}{4}$"

$14\frac{1}{4}$" $2\frac{1}{2}$" $2\frac{1}{2}$"

$10\frac{1}{8}$" 3"

SHELVES

$1\frac{5}{8}$"

$2\frac{1}{2}$" $\frac{7}{8}$" SHELVES HERE

85"

$2\frac{3}{4}$ SCALE IN INCHES

$\frac{1}{16}$" = 1"

$9\frac{1}{2}$"

$44\frac{1}{2}$"

$\frac{7}{8}$" $3\frac{3}{4}$"

$1\frac{1}{8}$"

1" $2\frac{5}{8}$"

$3\frac{1}{2}$"

$14\frac{1}{4}$"

$9\frac{15}{16}$"

$1\frac{5}{8}$"

4"

$9\frac{1}{2}$"

$20\frac{3}{8}$"

2

PIERCED TIN PANELS FOR PIE-SAFE
PIERCED TOWARD THE OUTSIDE
TO HELP KEEP INSECTS OUT
SOUTH UNION, KENTUCKY

TOP RAIL

$5\frac{1}{4}"$

$22\frac{1}{4}"$

$10\frac{1}{8}"$

$2\frac{1}{2}"$ $1\frac{5}{8}"$ $\frac{3}{8}"$ $2\frac{1}{2}"$

PANEL MOULDING

SCALE IN INCHES

$14\frac{1}{4}"$

PINE CUPBOARD CHEST
ANDREWS COLLECTION

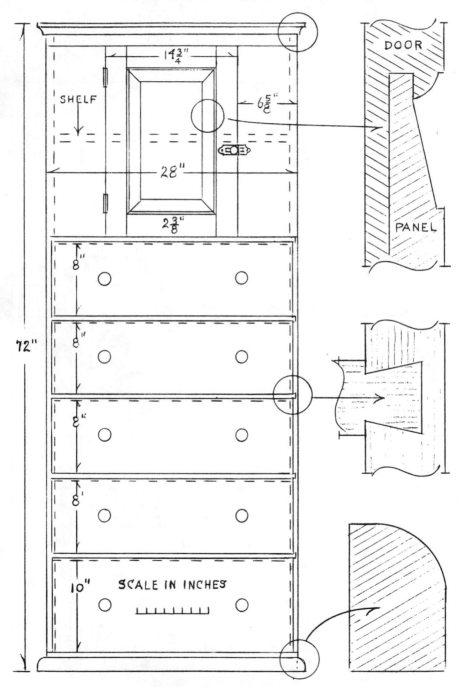

DOOR

SHELF

$14\frac{3}{4}$"

$6\frac{5}{8}$"

28"

$2\frac{3}{8}$"

PANEL

72"

8"

8"

8"

8"

10"

SCALE IN INCHES

4

PINE CUPBOARD CHEST
LIGHT-BROWN STAIN AND VARNISH
ANDREWS COLLECTION

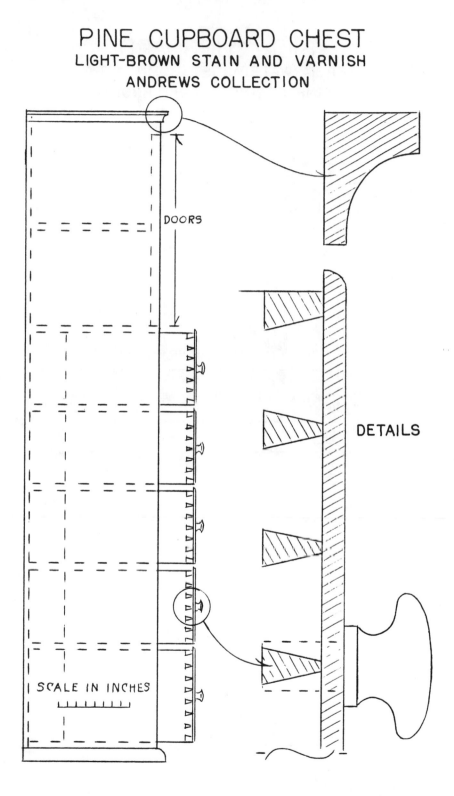

DOORS

DETAILS

SCALE IN INCHES

SILL CUPBOARD
FROM WATERVLIET COMMUNITY
PINE, STAINED LIGHT BROWN

FROM ANDREWS COLLECTION

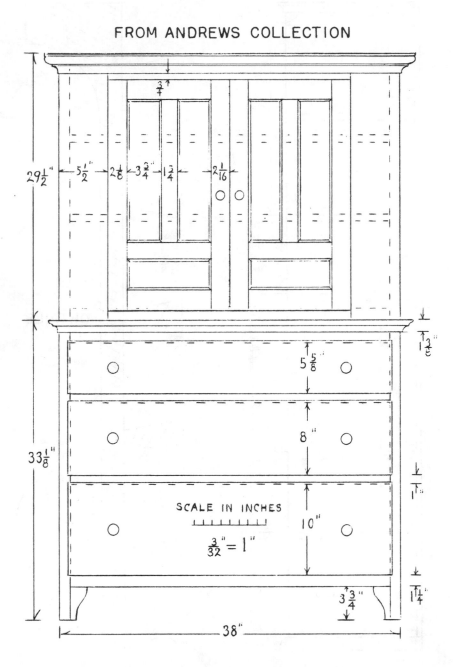

SCALE IN INCHES

$\frac{3}{32}" = 1"$

SILL CUPBOARD
WATERVLIET, N.Y.
PINE

ANDREWS COLLECTION

DETAILS

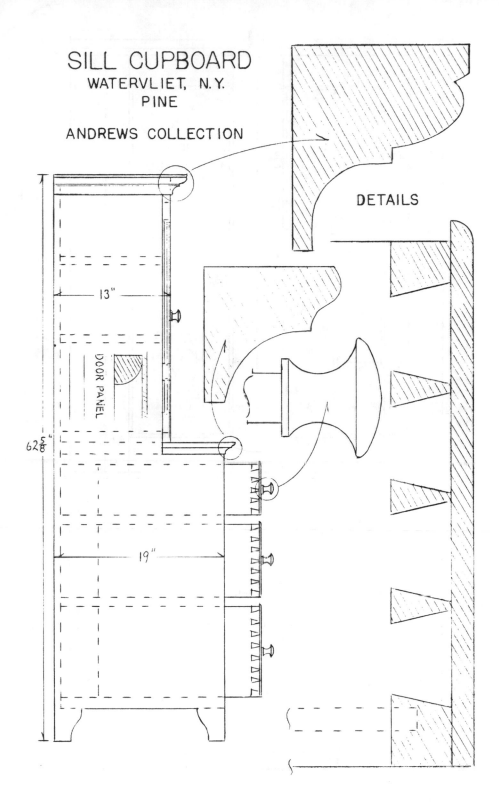

13"

DOOR PANEL

62⅝"

19"

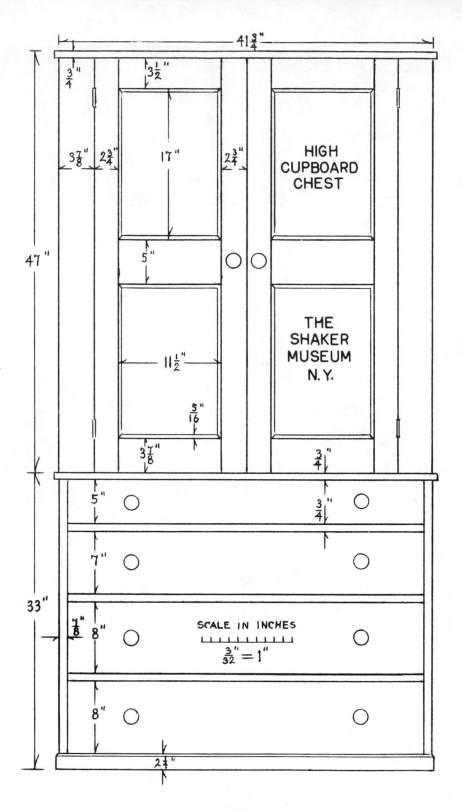

HIGH
CUPBOARD
CHEST

THE
SHAKER
MUSEUM
N.Y.

SCALE IN INCHES
$\frac{3}{32}$" = 1"

8

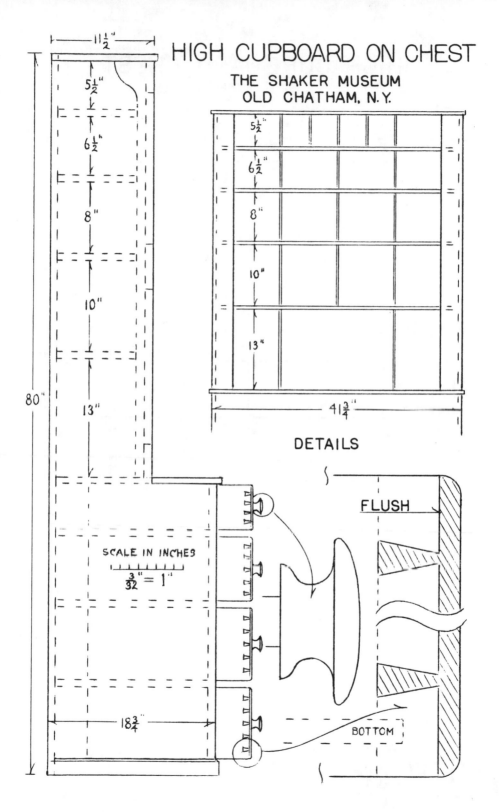

HIGH CUPBOARD ON CHEST

THE SHAKER MUSEUM
OLD CHATHAM, N.Y.

$11\frac{1}{2}$"

$5\frac{1}{2}$"

$6\frac{1}{2}$"

8"

10"

13"

80"

$5\frac{1}{2}$"

$6\frac{1}{2}$"

8"

10"

13"

$41\frac{3}{4}$"

DETAILS

SCALE IN INCHES

$\frac{3}{32}$" = 1"

$18\frac{3}{4}$"

FLUSH

BOTTOM

9

HIGH CUPBOARD CHEST

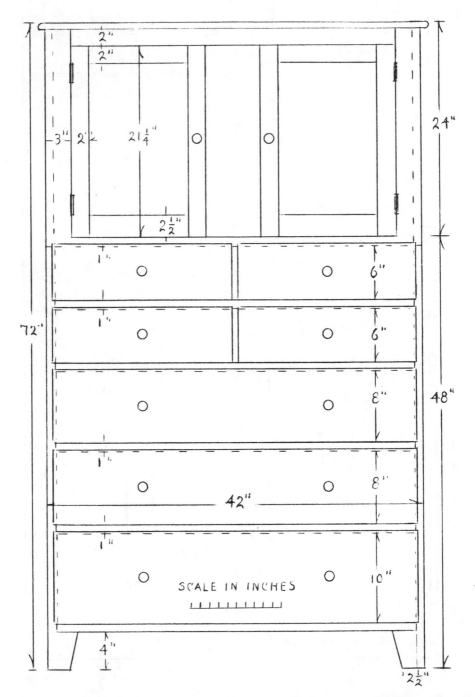

SCALE IN INCHES

CUPBOARD CHEST

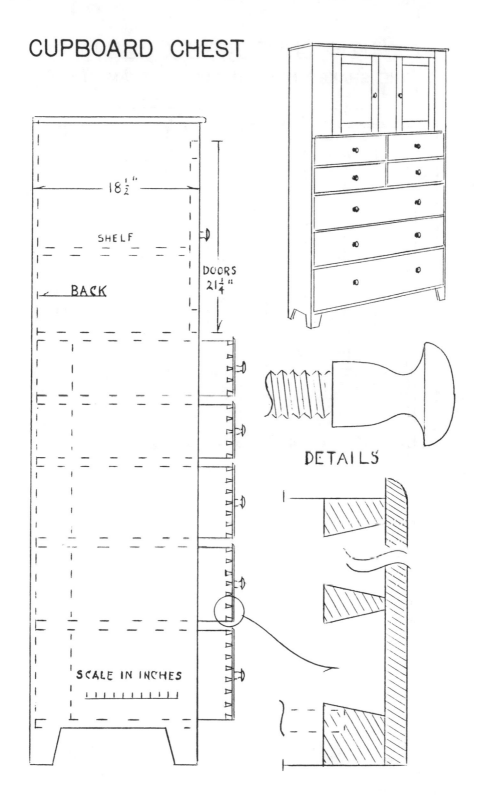

18½"

SHELF

BACK

DOORS
21¼"

DETAILS

SCALE IN INCHES

HIGH CUPBOARD CHEST
THE SHAKER MUSEUM, OLD CHATHAM, N.Y.

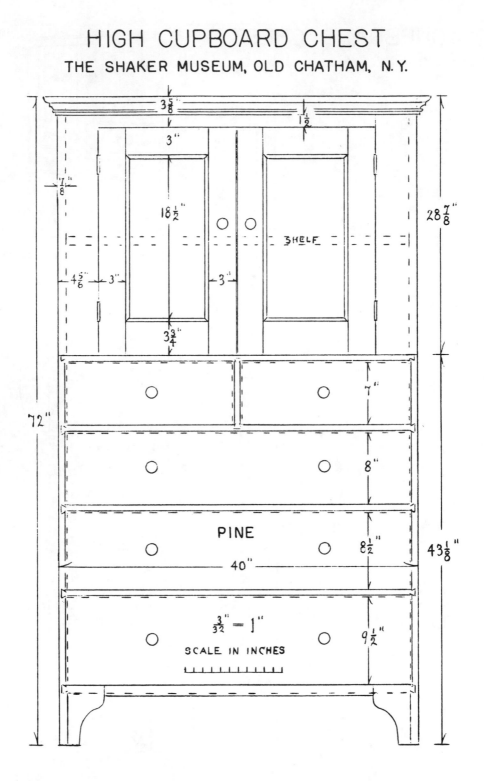

$3\frac{5}{8}$"

$1\frac{1}{2}$"

3"

$\frac{7}{8}$"

$18\frac{1}{2}$"

SHELF

$28\frac{7}{8}$"

$4\frac{5}{8}$" — 3"

3"

$3\frac{3}{4}$"

7"

8"

PINE

$8\frac{1}{2}$"

40"

$43\frac{1}{8}$"

72"

$\frac{3}{32}$" = 1"

SCALE IN INCHES

$9\frac{1}{2}$"

HIGH CUPBOARD CHEST
THE SHAKER MUSEUM, OLD CHATHAM, N.Y.

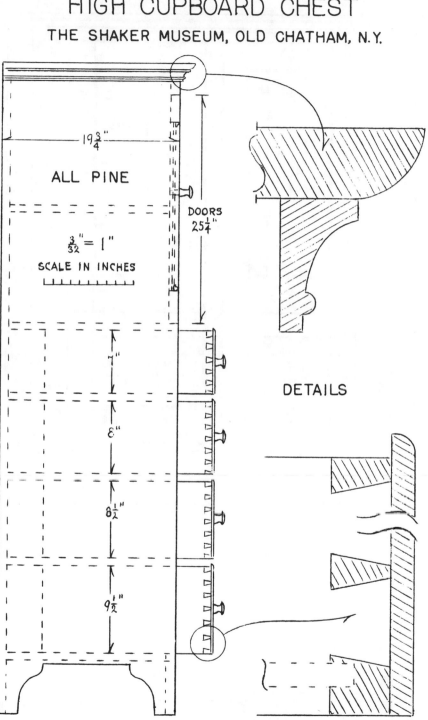

$19\frac{3}{4}$"

ALL PINE

DOORS $25\frac{1}{4}$"

$\frac{3}{32}$" = 1"

SCALE IN INCHES

7"

8"

$8\frac{1}{2}$"

$9\frac{1}{2}$"

DETAILS

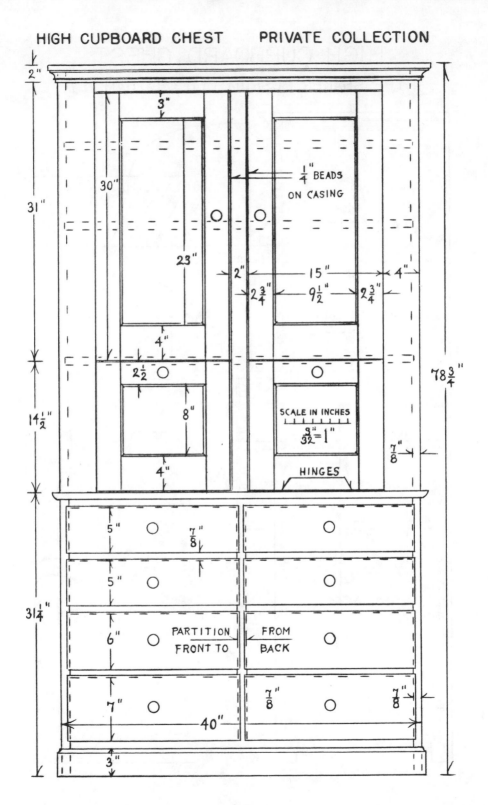

HIGH CUPBOARD CHEST

PRIVATE COLLECTION

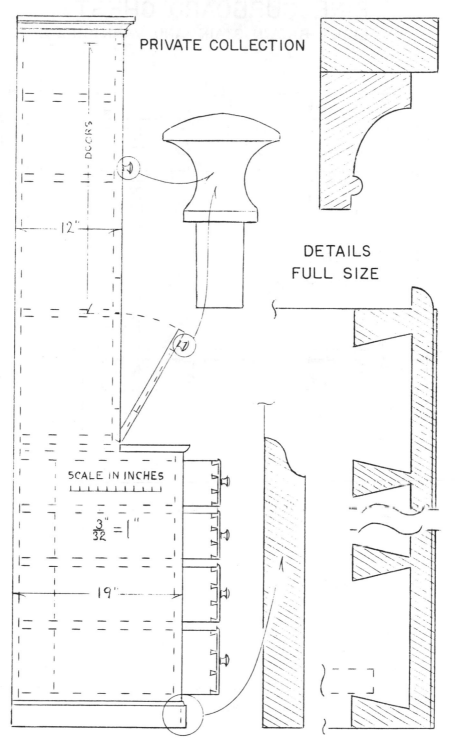

DOORS

12"

DETAILS
FULL SIZE

SCALE IN INCHES

$\frac{3"}{32} = 1"$

19"

15

PINE CUPBOARD CHEST
LIGHT-BROWN STAIN AND VARNISH

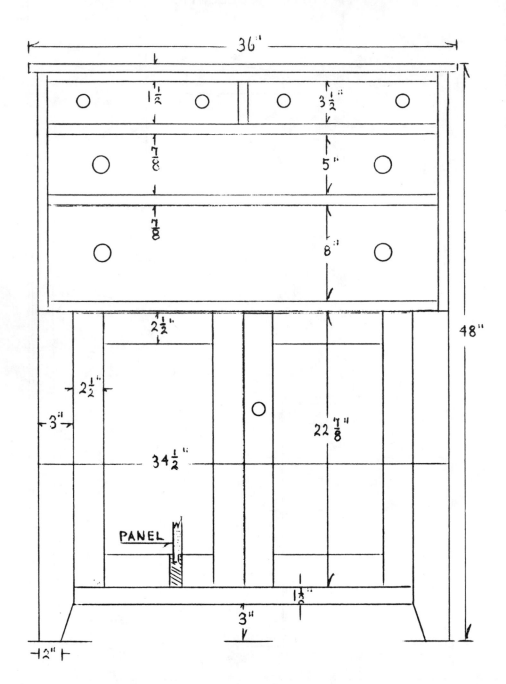

PINE CUPBOARD CHEST
LIGHT-BROWN STAIN AND VARNISH

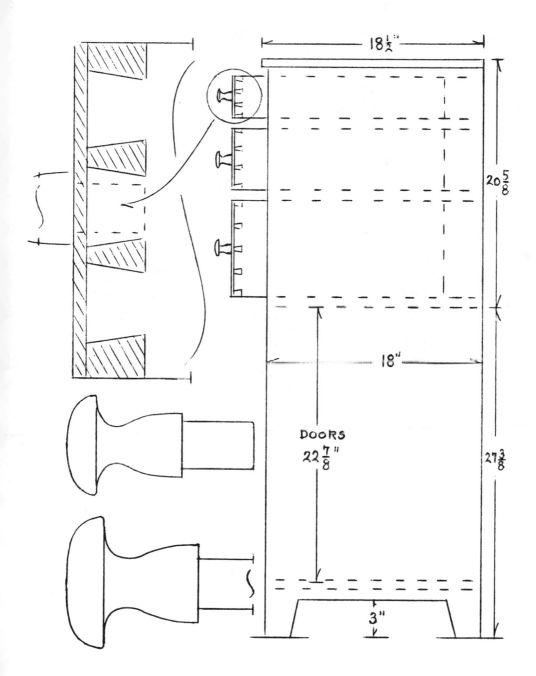

TAILORESSES' SHOP COUNTER

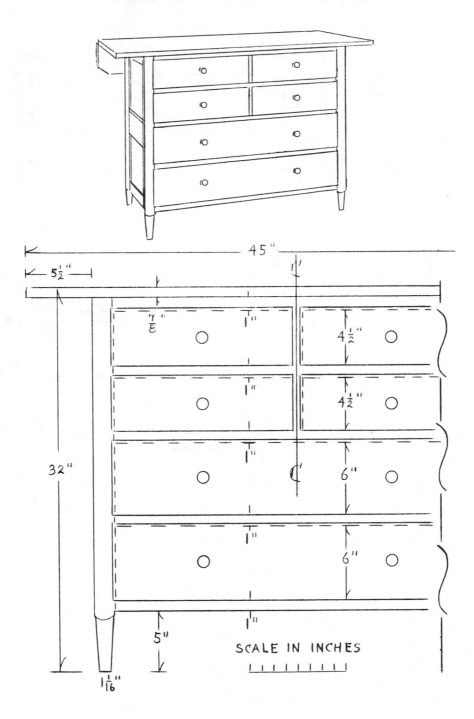

45"

5½"

¾"
3"

1"

4½"

1"

4½"

1"

1'

32"

6"

6"

1"

1"

5"

1¹⁄₁₆"

SCALE IN INCHES

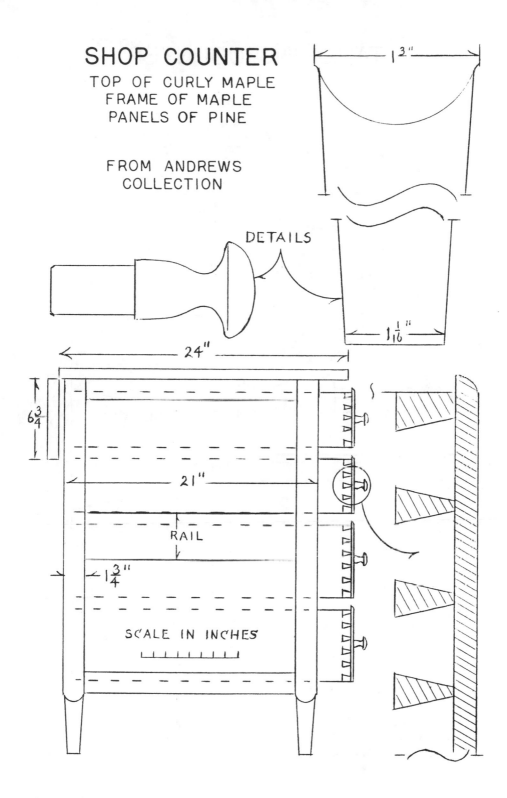

SHOP COUNTER

TOP OF CURLY MAPLE
FRAME OF MAPLE
PANELS OF PINE

FROM ANDREWS
COLLECTION

$1\frac{3}{}$"

DETAILS

$1\frac{1}{16}$"

24"

$6\frac{3}{4}$

21"

RAIL

$1\frac{3}{4}$"

SCALE IN INCHES

19

TAILORING COUNTER

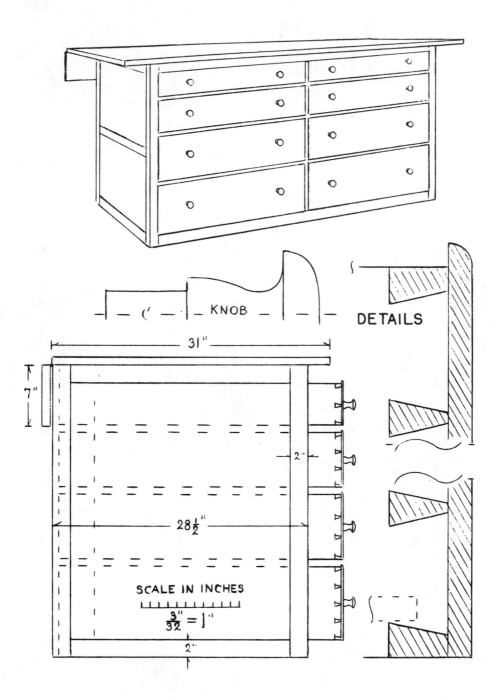

KNOB

DETAILS

31"

7"

2"

28½"

SCALE IN INCHES

$\frac{3"}{32} = 1"$

2"

TAILORING COUNTER
A COMBINATION OF TABLE
AND CHEST OF DRAWERS

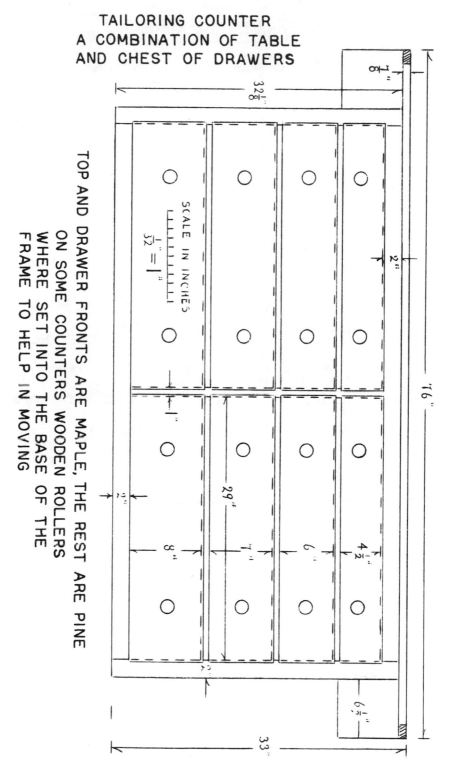

TOP AND DRAWER FRONTS ARE MAPLE, THE REST ARE PINE
ON SOME COUNTERS WOODEN ROLLERS
WHERE SET INTO THE BASE OF THE
FRAME TO HELP IN MOVING

SCALE IN INCHES
$\frac{1}{32}" = 1"$

STORAGE BENCH ca. 1800

THE SHAKER MUSEUM, OLD CHATHAM, N.Y.

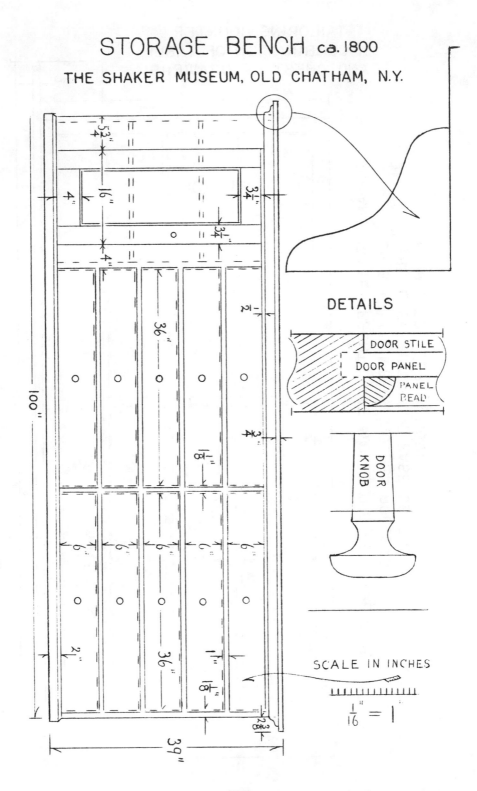

DETAILS

DOOR STILE

DOOR PANEL

PANEL BEAD

DOOR KNOB

SCALE IN INCHES

$\frac{1}{16}" = 1$

STORAGE BENCH ca. 1800
PINE, PAINTED BLUE
FROM CANTERBURY, N. H.

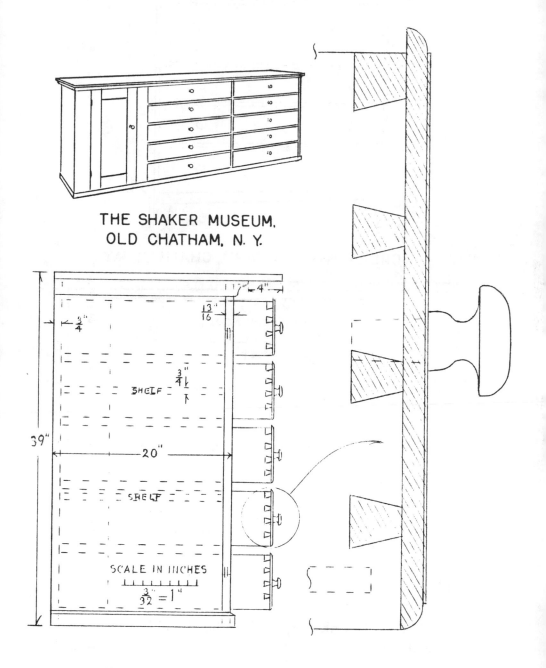

THE SHAKER MUSEUM.
OLD CHATHAM, N. Y.

SCALE IN INCHES

$\frac{3}{32}" = 1"$

CHEST OF DRAWERS
FROM NEW LEBANON

GREEN WILLOW FARM, CHATHAM N.Y.

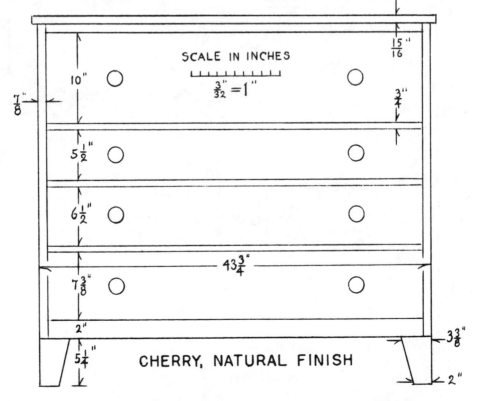

SCALE IN INCHES

$\frac{3}{32}" = 1"$

$\frac{15}{16}"$

$10"$

$\frac{7}{8}"$

$\frac{3}{4}"$

$5\frac{1}{2}"$

$6\frac{1}{2}"$

$43\frac{3}{4}"$

$7\frac{3}{8}"$

$2"$

$3\frac{3}{8}"$

$5\frac{1}{4}"$

CHERRY, NATURAL FINISH

$2"$

24

CHEST OF DRAWERS
FROM NEW LEBANON

CHERRY, FINISHED NATURAL

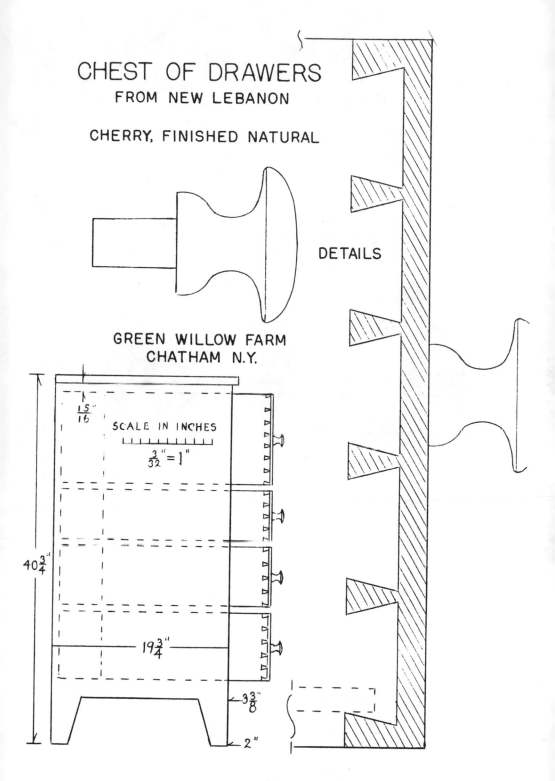

DETAILS

GREEN WILLOW FARM
CHATHAM N.Y.

$\frac{15}{16}$"

SCALE IN INCHES

$\frac{3}{32}$" = 1"

$40\frac{3}{4}$"

$19\frac{3}{4}$"

$3\frac{3}{8}$"

2"

CHEST
OF
DRAWERS
FROM NEW LEBANON

PRIVATE COLLECTION

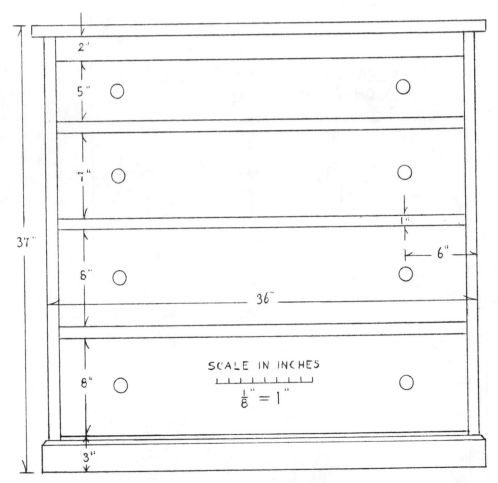

SCALE IN INCHES

$\frac{1}{8}" = 1"$

CHEST OF DRAWERS
FROM NEW LEBANON
CHERRY AND PINE

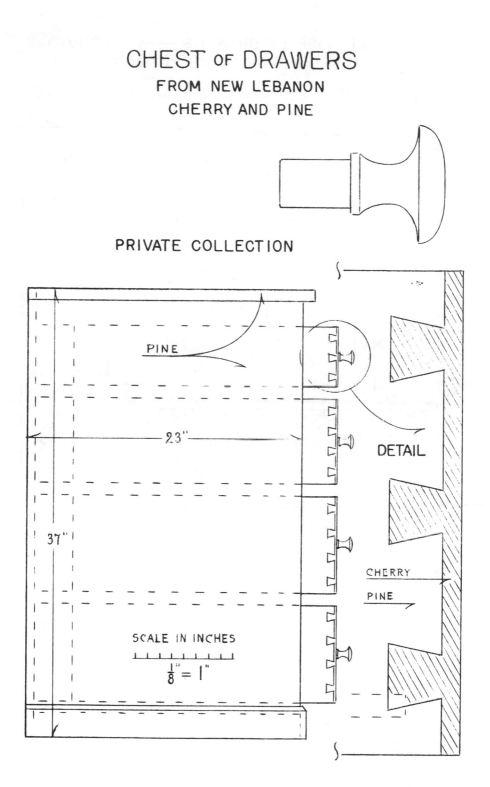

PRIVATE COLLECTION

PINE

23"

37"

DETAIL

CHERRY

PINE

SCALE IN INCHES

$\frac{1}{8}" = 1"$

SMALL CASE OF DRAWERS — BUTTERNUT
FROM ENFIELD CONN. 1849

BOSTON MUSEUM OF FINE ARTS, BOSTON MASS.

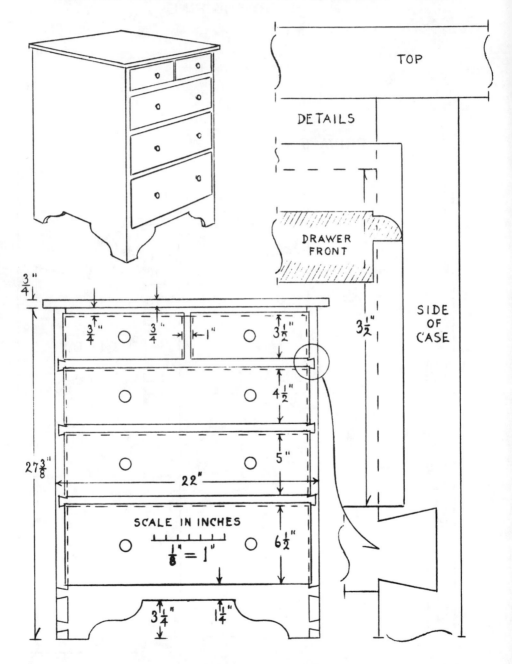

TOP

DETAILS

DRAWER FRONT

SIDE OF CASE

SCALE IN INCHES

$\frac{1}{8}" = 1"$

CASE OF DRAWERS — BUTTERNUT
FROM ENFIELD CONN. 1849

BOSTON MUSEUM OF FINE ARTS, BOSTON MASS.

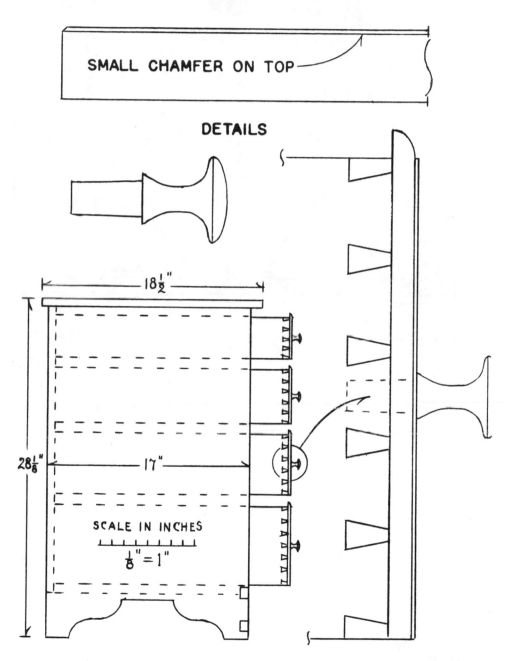

SMALL CHAMFER ON TOP

DETAILS

$18\frac{1}{2}$"

$28\frac{1}{8}$"

17"

SCALE IN INCHES

$\frac{1}{8}$" = 1"

SHAKER UPRIGHT DESK
MAPLE CASE – CHERRY LEGS

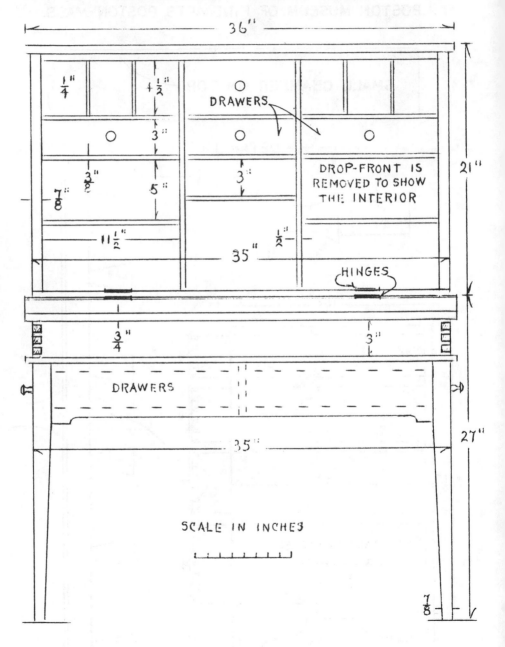

SCALE IN INCHES

SHAKER UPRIGHT DESK
MAPLE CASE — CHERRY LEGS

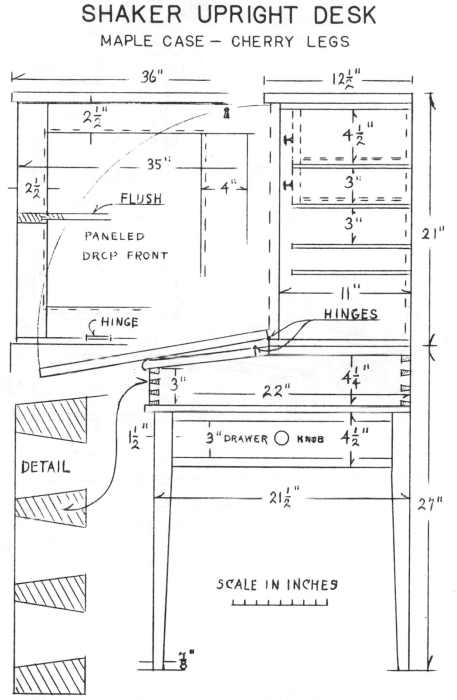

36" 12½"

2½"

4½"

35"

4"

2½"

FLUSH

3"

PANELED
DROP FRONT

3"

21"

11"

HINGES

HINGE

3"

4¼"

22"

1½"

3" DRAWER ◯ KNOB 4½"

DETAIL

21½"

27"

SCALE IN INCHES

⅞"

DETAILS ON NEXT PAGE

DETAILS OF UPRIGHT DESK

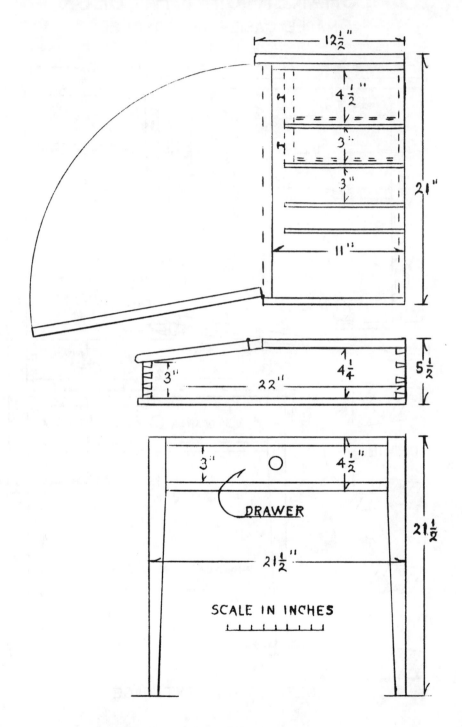

SCALE IN INCHES

DETAILS OF UPRIGHT DESK

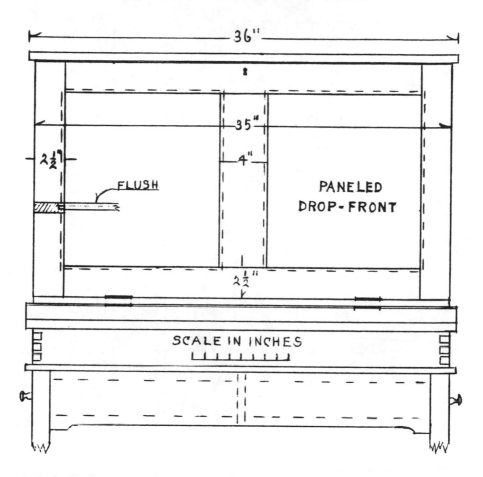

36"

35"

4"

2½"

2½"

FLUSH

PANELED
DROP-FRONT

SCALE IN INCHES

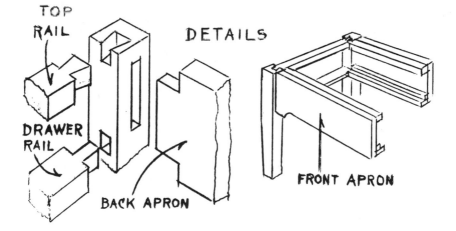

TOP
RAIL

DETAILS

DRAWER
RAIL

BACK APRON

FRONT APRON

SCHOOL DESK
OAK AND CHERRY

$\frac{1}{8}" = 1"$

SCALE IN INCHES

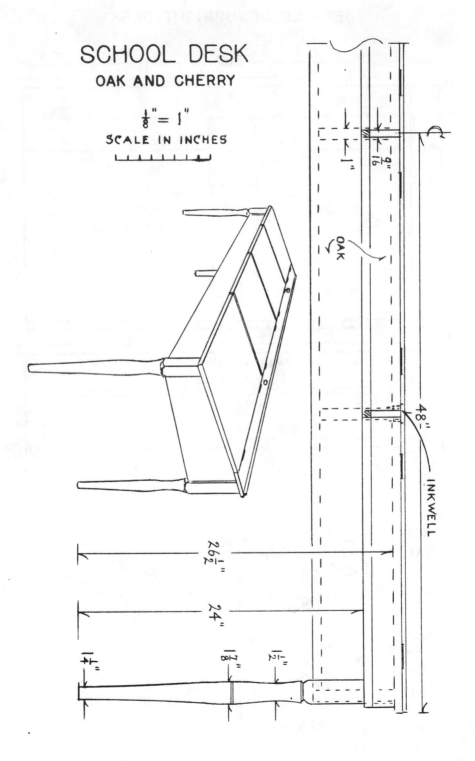

OAK

INKWELL

$\frac{9}{16}$"

1"

48"

$26\frac{1}{2}$"

24"

$1\frac{1}{4}$"

$1\frac{7}{8}$"

$1\frac{1}{2}$"

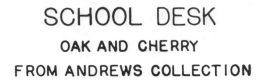

SCHOOL DESK

OAK AND CHERRY

FROM ANDREWS COLLECTION

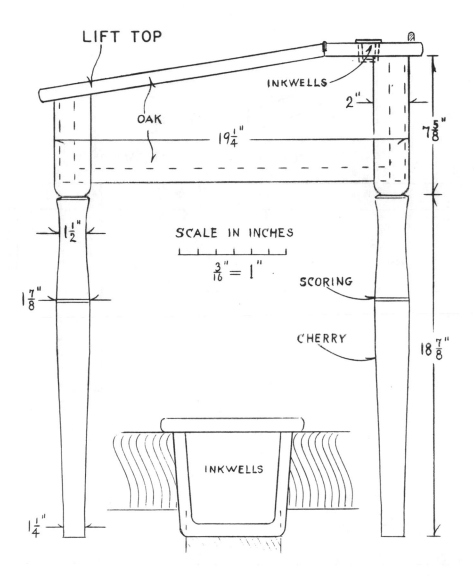

LIFT TOP

INKWELLS

OAK

$19\frac{1}{4}$"

2"

$7\frac{5}{8}$"

$1\frac{1}{2}$"

SCALE IN INCHES

$\frac{3}{16}$" $= 1$"

SCORING

$1\frac{7}{8}$"

CHERRY

$18\frac{7}{8}$"

INKWELLS

$1\frac{1}{4}$"

TABLE DESK
FROM CANTERBURY N.H.

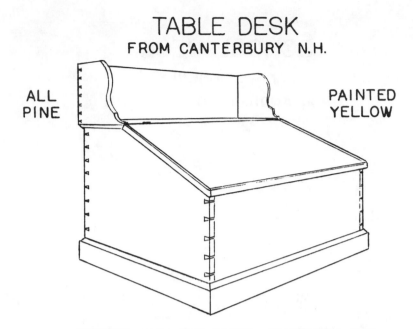

ALL
PINE

PAINTED
YELLOW

GREEN WILLOW FARM, CHATHAM N.Y.

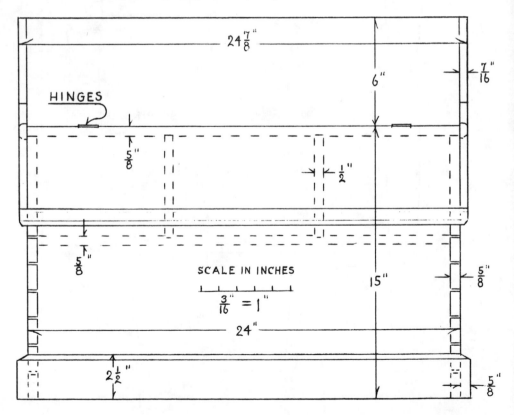

HINGES

$24\frac{7}{8}$"

$\frac{7}{16}$"

6"

$\frac{5}{8}$"

$\frac{1}{2}$"

$\frac{5}{8}$"

$\frac{5}{8}$"

15"

SCALE IN INCHES

$\frac{3}{16}$" = 1"

24"

$2\frac{1}{2}$"

$\frac{5}{8}$"

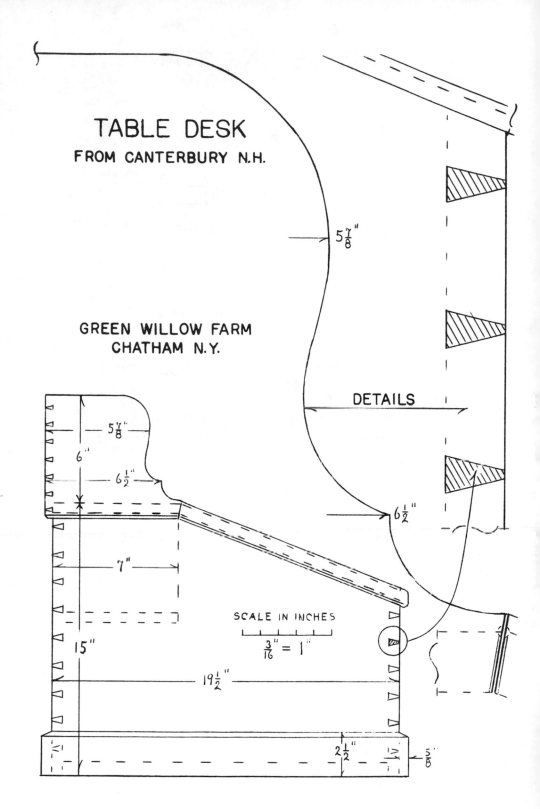

TABLE DESK
FROM CANTERBURY N.H.

GREEN WILLOW FARM
CHATHAM N.Y.

DETAILS

$5\frac{7}{8}$"

$6\frac{1}{2}$"

$5\frac{7}{8}$"

$6\frac{1}{2}$"

6"

7"

15"

$19\frac{1}{2}$"

SCALE IN INCHES

$\frac{3}{16}$" = 1"

$2\frac{1}{2}$"

$\frac{5}{8}$"

PINE SEWING STAND

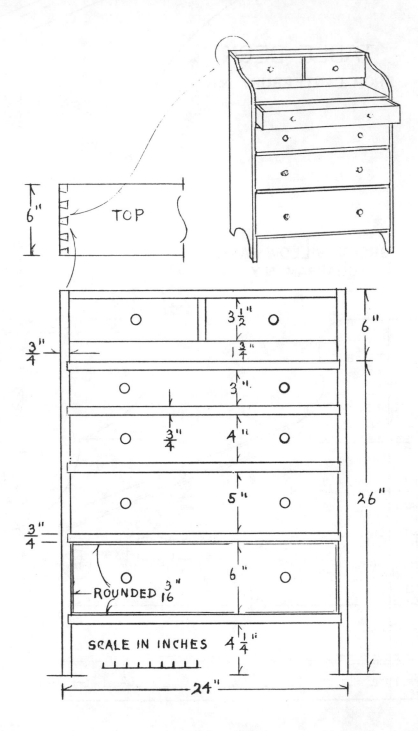

TOP

6"

3/4"

3 1/2"

1 3/4"

6"

3"

3/4"

4"

5"

26"

ROUNDED 3/16"

6"

SCALE IN INCHES   4 1/4"

24"

PINE SEWING STAND
LIGHT-BROWN STAIN AND VARNISH

WRITING OR CUTTING BOARD SET IN TOP
OF LONG DRAWER, REMOVABLE AT WILL

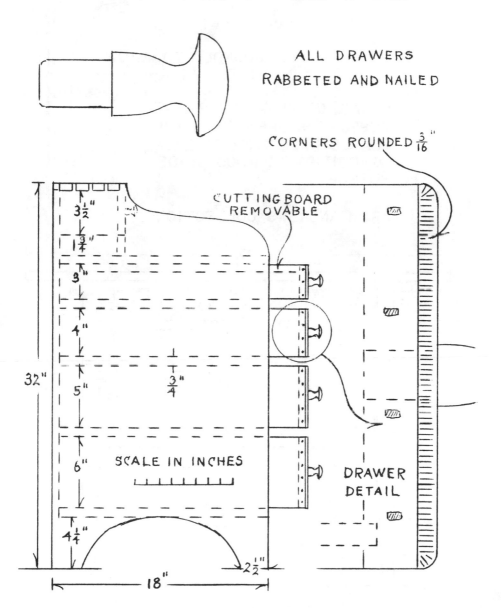

ALL DRAWERS
RABBETED AND NAILED

CORNERS ROUNDED $\frac{3}{16}$"

CUTTING BOARD
REMOVABLE

$3\frac{1}{2}$"

$1\frac{3}{4}$"

3"

4"

32"

5"

$\frac{3}{4}$

6"

SCALE IN INCHES

DRAWER
DETAIL

$4\frac{1}{4}$"

$2\frac{1}{2}$"

18"

SEWING TABLE

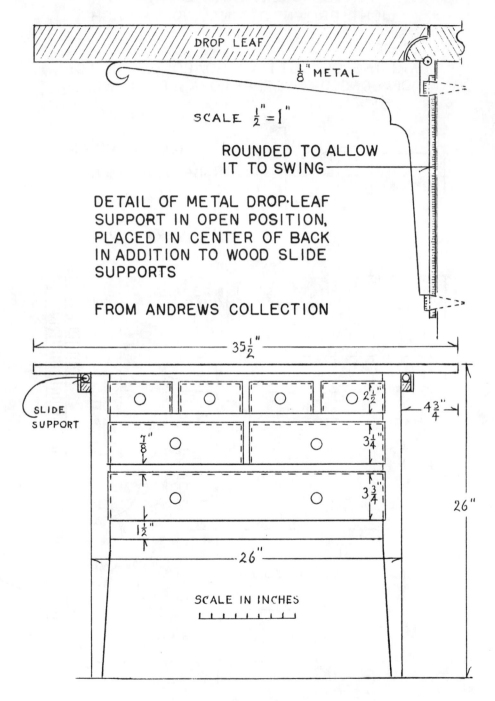

DROP LEAF

$\frac{1}{8}$" METAL

SCALE $\frac{1}{2}$" = 1"

ROUNDED TO ALLOW
IT TO SWING

DETAIL OF METAL DROP-LEAF
SUPPORT IN OPEN POSITION,
PLACED IN CENTER OF BACK
IN ADDITION TO WOOD SLIDE
SUPPORTS

FROM ANDREWS COLLECTION

$35\frac{1}{2}$"

SLIDE
SUPPORT

$2\frac{1}{2}$"

$4\frac{3}{4}$"

$\frac{7}{8}$"

$3\frac{1}{4}$"

$3\frac{3}{4}$"

26"

$1\frac{1}{2}$"

26"

SCALE IN INCHES

SEWING TABLE
CHERRY TOP AND FRAME PINE PANELS
ANDREWS COLLECTION

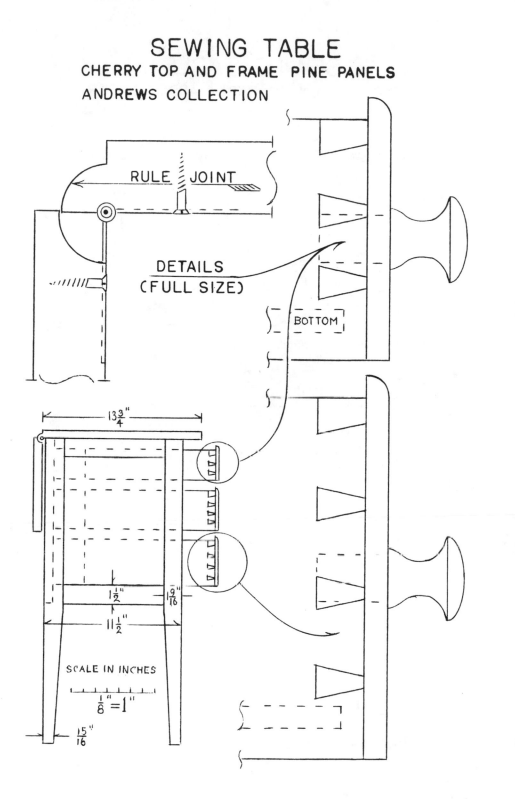

RULE JOINT

DETAILS
(FULL SIZE)

BOTTOM

$13\frac{3}{4}$"

$1\frac{1}{2}$" $\frac{9}{16}$"

$11\frac{1}{2}$"

SCALE IN INCHES

$\frac{1}{8}$"$=1$"

$\frac{15}{16}$"

SEWING TABLE
TOP SECTION PROBABLY ADDED LATER

FROM NEW LEBANON   PRIVATE COLLECTION

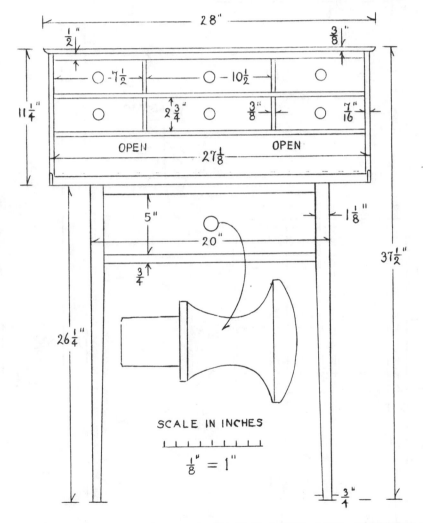

SCALE IN INCHES

$\frac{1}{8}" = 1"$

ALL DRAWER FRONTS AND TABLE LEGS ARE CHERRY

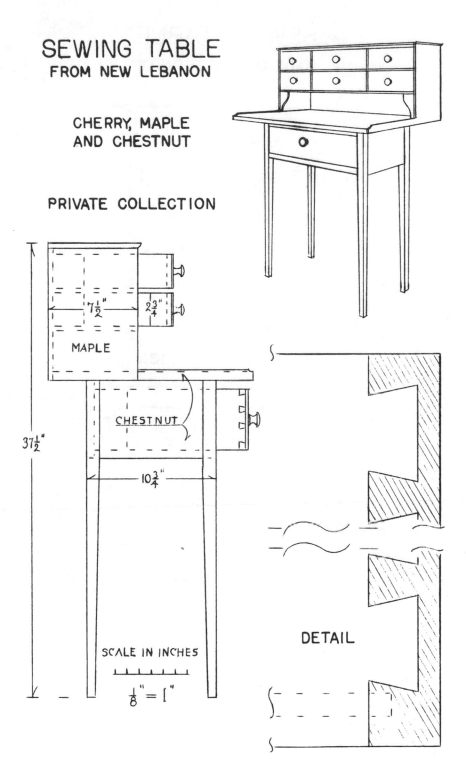

SEWING TABLE
FROM NEW LEBANON

CHERRY, MAPLE
AND CHESTNUT

PRIVATE COLLECTION

7½"

2¾"

MAPLE

CHESTNUT

37½"

10¾"

DETAIL

SCALE IN INCHES

⅛" = 1"

SEWING TABLE
MADE OF BUTTERNUT

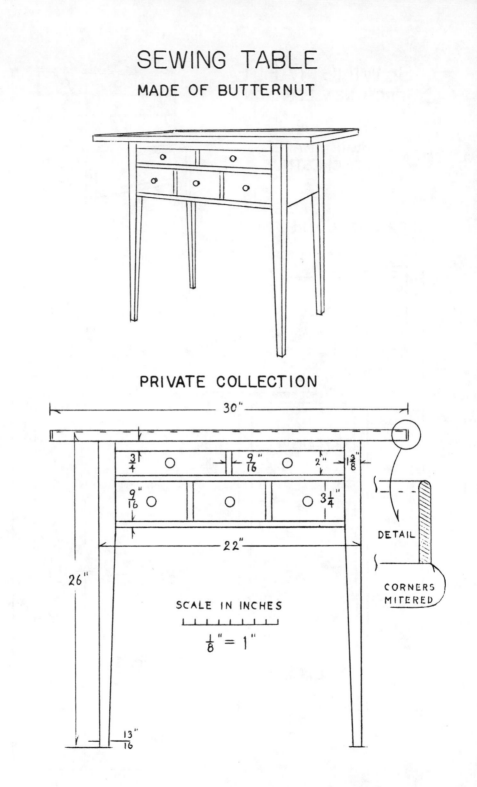

PRIVATE COLLECTION

30"

$\frac{3}{4}$ $\frac{9}{16}$" 2" $\frac{3}{8}$"

$\frac{9}{16}$" $3\frac{1}{4}$"

DETAIL

CORNERS
MITERED

22"

26"

SCALE IN INCHES

$\frac{1}{8}$" = 1"

$\frac{13}{16}$"

SEWING TABLE
MADE OF BUTTERNUT

PRIVATE COLLECTION

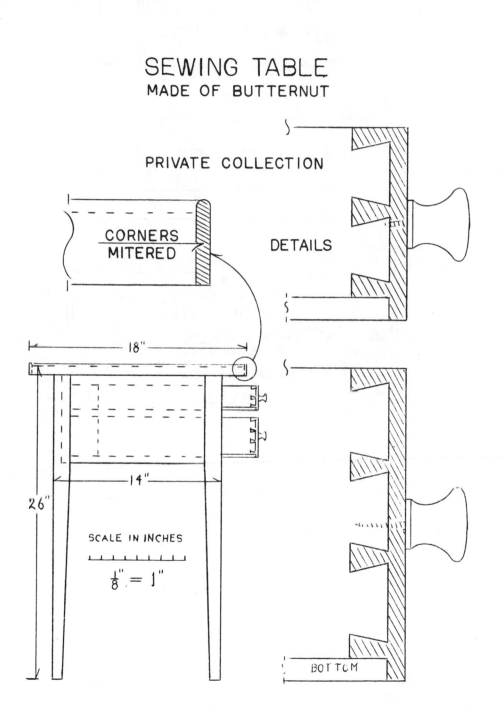

CORNERS
MITERED

DETAILS

18"

14"

26"

SCALE IN INCHES

$\frac{1}{8}" = 1"$

BOTTOM

PINE WASH-STAND
NEW LEBANON N.Y.

MUSEUM OF FINE ARTS, BOSTON, MASS.

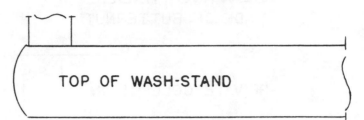

TOP OF WASH-STAND

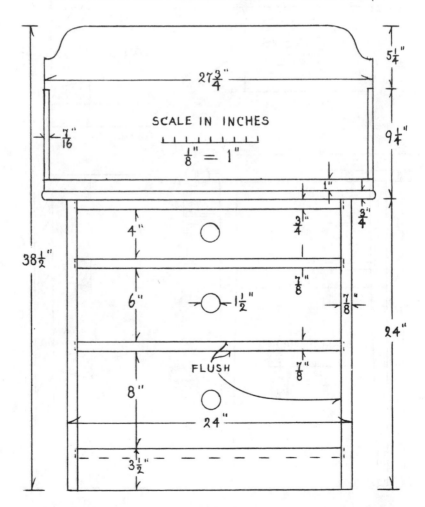

SCALE IN INCHES

$\frac{1}{8}" = 1"$

PINE WASH-STAND
NEW LEBANON N.Y.
MUSEUM OF FINE ARTS, BOSTON, MASS.

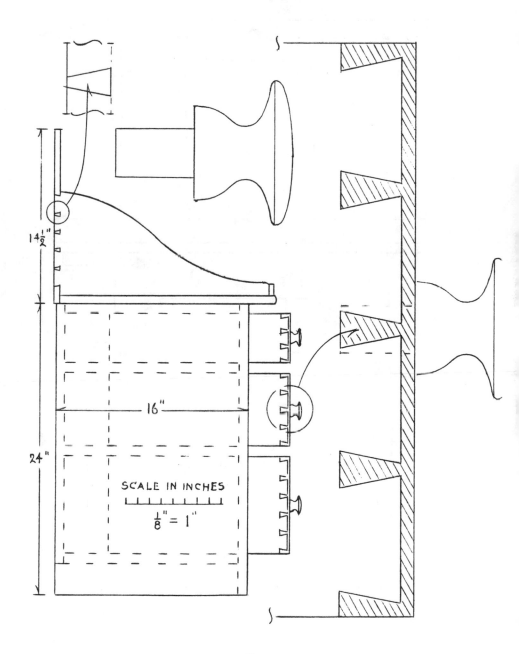

SCALE IN INCHES

$\frac{1}{8}" = 1"$

DINING TABLE
CANTERBURY, N.H.
BIRCH WITH TOP OF BUTTERNUT
THE SHAKER MUSEUM, OLD CHATHAM, N.Y.

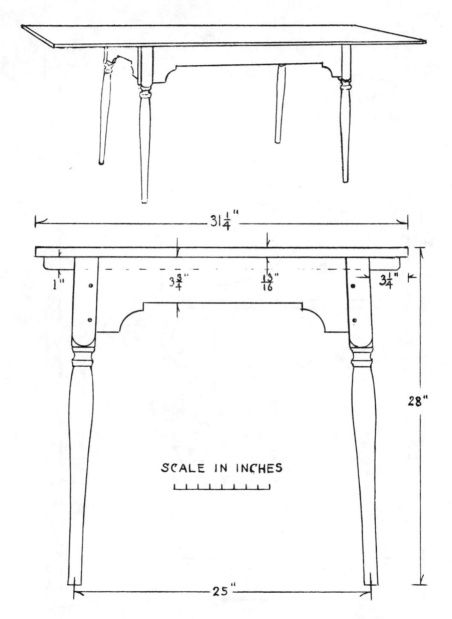

$31\frac{1}{4}$"

1"

$3\frac{3}{4}$"

$\frac{13}{16}$"

$3\frac{1}{4}$"

28"

SCALE IN INCHES

25"

48

DINING TABLE
CANTERBURY, N. H.
THE SHAKER MUSEUM, OLD CHATHAM, N.Y.

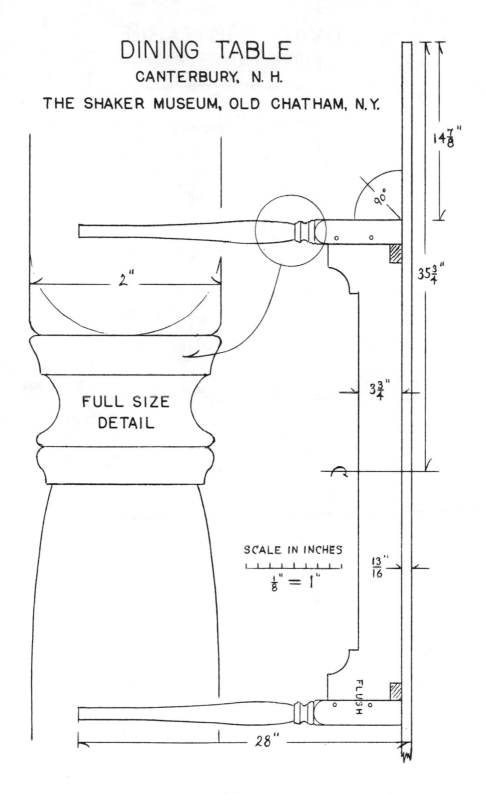

$14\frac{7}{8}$"

90°

2"

$35\frac{3}{4}$"

FULL SIZE
DETAIL

$3\frac{3}{4}$"

SCALE IN INCHES

$\frac{1}{8}$" = 1"

$\frac{13}{16}$"

FLUSH

28"

OVAL-TOP TABLE
BIRCH WITH PINE TOP

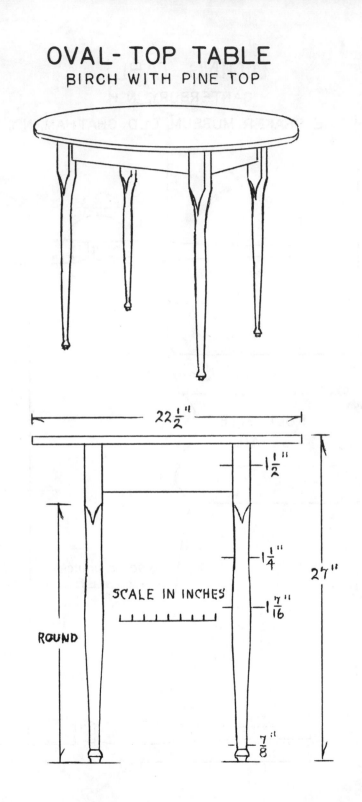

22½"

1½"

1¼"

1$\frac{7}{16}$"

SCALE IN INCHES

ROUND

27"

$\frac{7}{8}$"

OVAL-TOP TABLE
BIRCH WITH PINE TOP

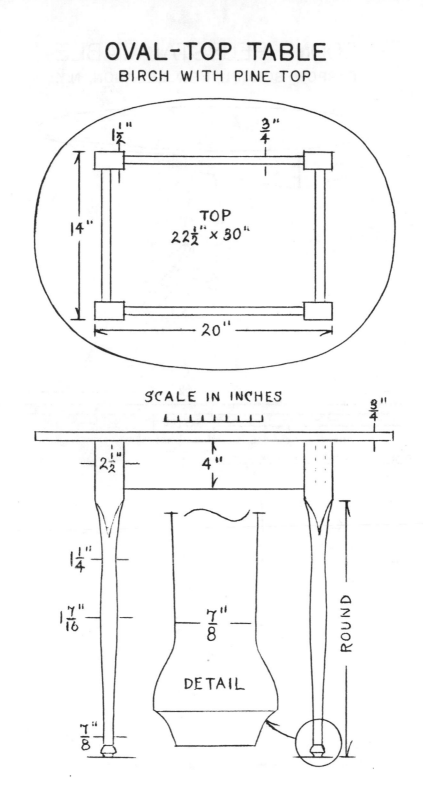

TOP
$22\frac{1}{2}" \times 30"$

$1\frac{1}{2}"$

$\frac{3}{4}"$

14"

20"

SCALE IN INCHES

$\frac{3}{4}"$

$2\frac{1}{2}"$

4"

$1\frac{1}{4}"$

$1\frac{7}{16}"$

$\frac{7}{8}"$

ROUND

$\frac{7}{8}"$

DETAIL

ROUND PEDESTAL TABLE
DARROW SCHOOL, NEW LEBANON, N.Y.

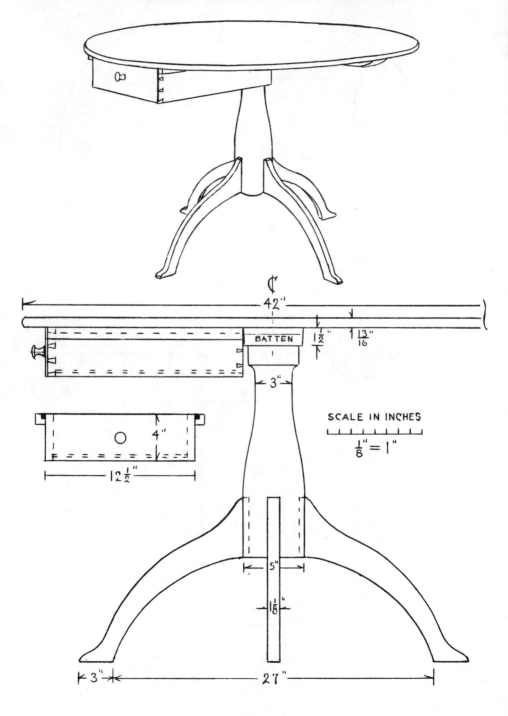

42"

BATTEN

$1\frac{1}{2}$"

$1\frac{13}{16}$"

3"

4"

$12\frac{1}{2}$"

SCALE IN INCHES

$\frac{1}{8}$" = 1"

5"

$1\frac{1}{8}$"

3"

27"

PEDESTAL TABLE
DARROW SCHOOL, NEW LEBANON, N.Y.

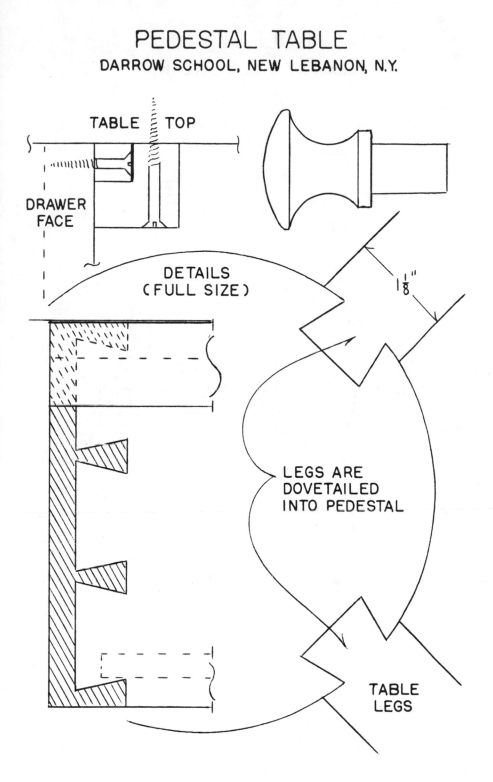

TABLE TOP

DRAWER
FACE

DETAILS
(FULL SIZE)

$1\frac{1}{8}$"

LEGS ARE
DOVETAILED
INTO PEDESTAL

TABLE
LEGS

CANDLESTAND
PLEASANT HILL, KENTUCKY

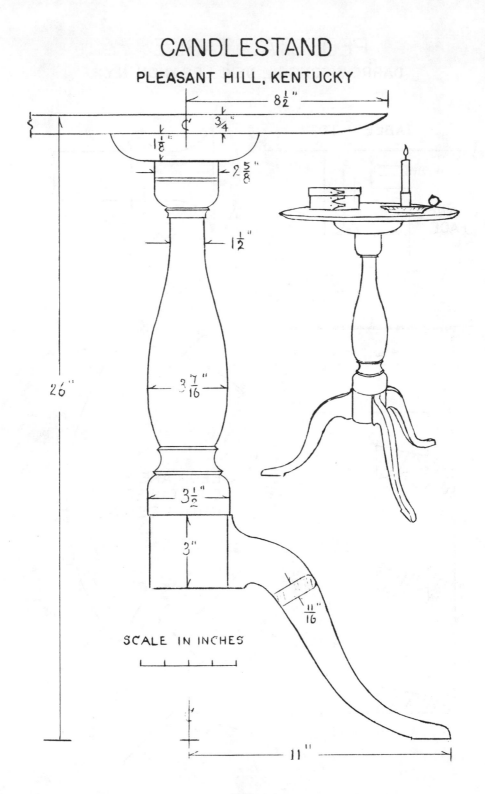

SCALE IN INCHES

CANDLESTAND
FROM MT. LEBANON

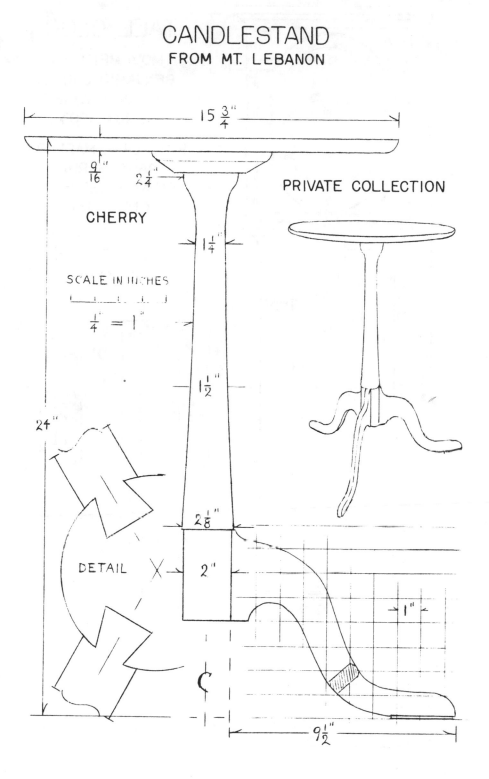

15 ¾"

9/16"

2 ¼"

PRIVATE COLLECTION

CHERRY

1 ¼"

SCALE IN INCHES

¼" = 1"

1 ½"

24"

DETAIL   X

2 ⅛"

2"

1"

C

9 ½"

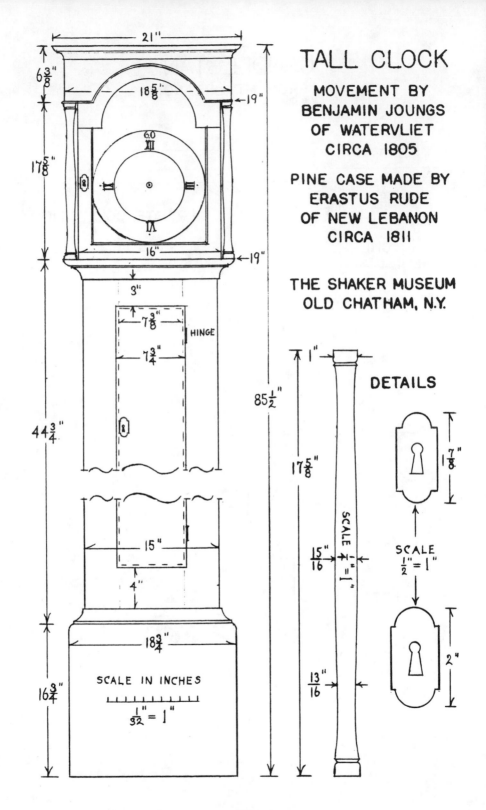

TALL CLOCK

MOVEMENT BY
BENJAMIN JOUNGS
OF WATERVLIET
CIRCA 1805

PINE CASE MADE BY
ERASTUS RUDE
OF NEW LEBANON
CIRCA 1811

THE SHAKER MUSEUM
OLD CHATHAM, N.Y.

DETAILS

SCALE
$\frac{1}{2}$" = 1"

SCALE IN INCHES

$\frac{1}{32}$" = 1"

HINGE

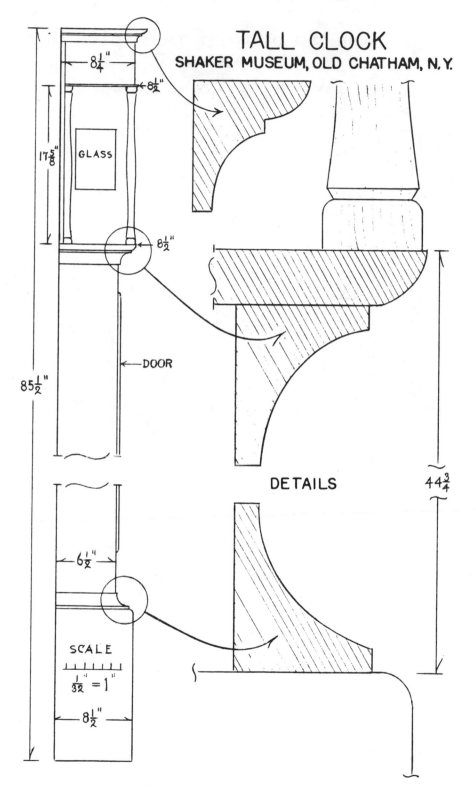

TALL CLOCK
SHAKER MUSEUM, OLD CHATHAM, N.Y.

8¼"

8½"

17⅝"

GLASS

8½"

85½"

DOOR

DETAILS

44¾

6½"

SCALE

$\frac{1}{32}$" = 1"

8½"

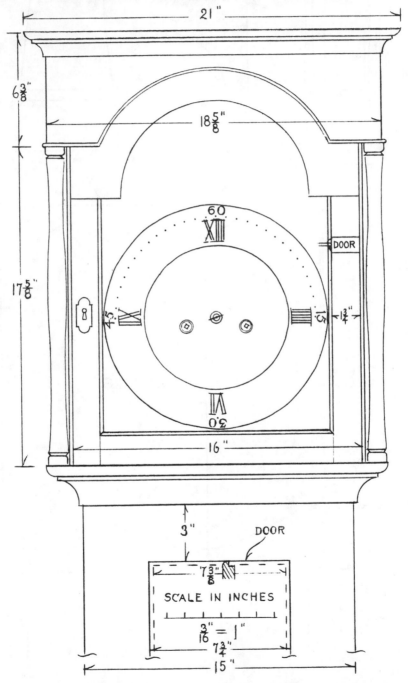

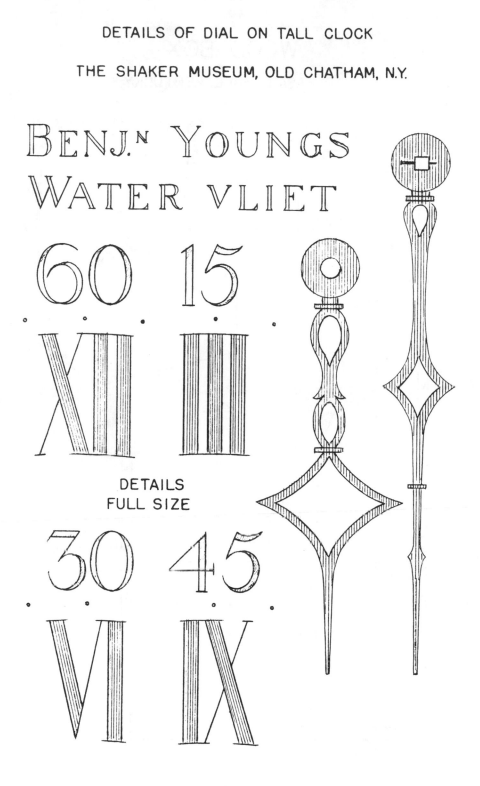

BENJ.ᴺ YOUNGS
WATER VLIET
60   15
XII III

DETAILS
FULL SIZE

30   45
VI   IX

WOOD BOX

PLEASANT HILL, KENTUCKY

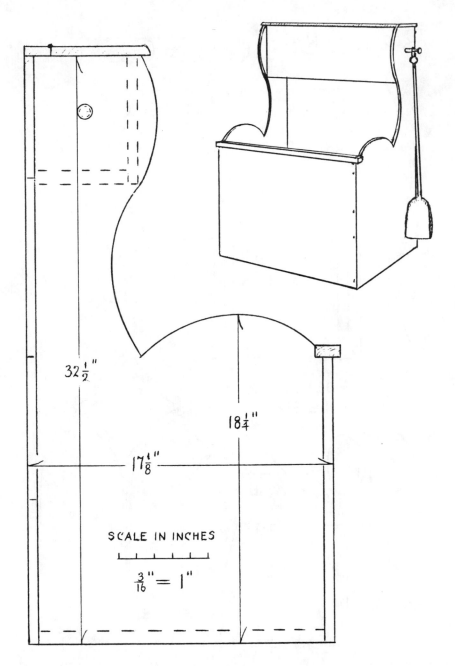

$32\frac{1}{2}''$

$18\frac{1}{4}''$

$17\frac{1}{8}''$

SCALE IN INCHES

$\frac{3}{16}'' = 1''$

WOOD BOX

PLEASANT HILL, KENTUCKY

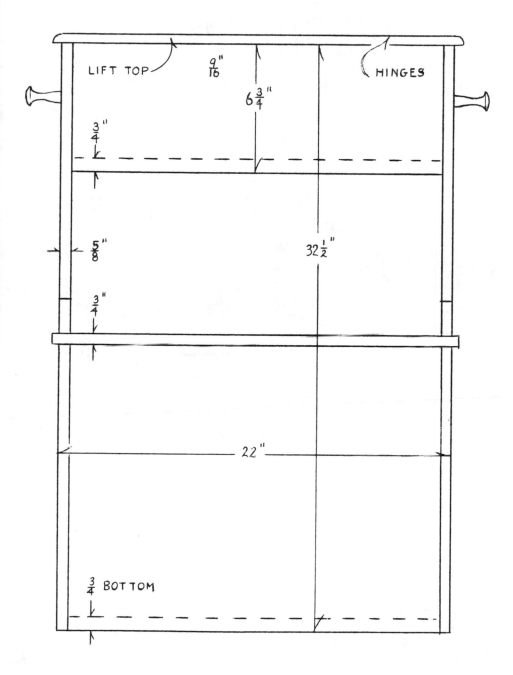

LIFT TOP

$\frac{9}{16}$"

HINGES

$6\frac{3}{4}$"

$\frac{3}{4}$"

$\frac{5}{8}$"

$\frac{3}{4}$"

$32\frac{1}{2}$"

22"

$\frac{3}{4}$ BOTTOM

CANTERBURY SETTEE
THE SHAKER MUSEUM   OLD CHATHAM, N. Y.

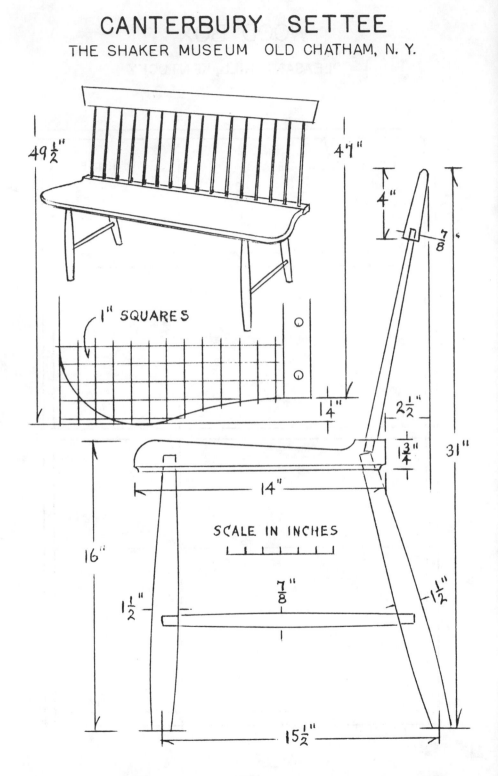

49½"

4'1"

4"

⅞"

1" SQUARES

2½"

1¾"

31"

1¼"

14"

SCALE IN INCHES

16"

⅞"

1½"

1½"

15½"

CANTERBURY SETTEE

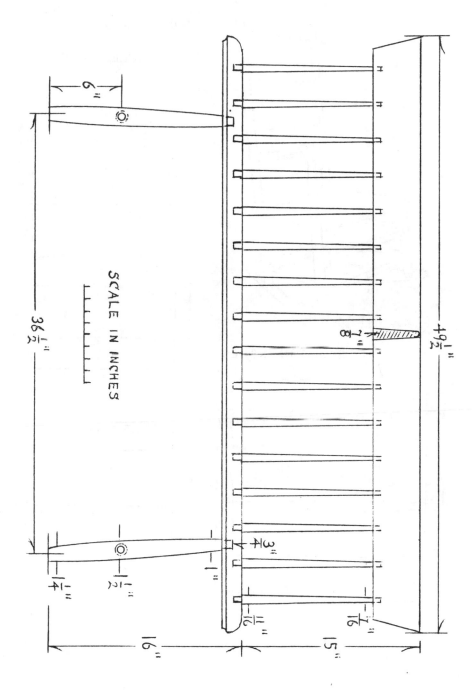

SCALE IN INCHES

$36\frac{1}{2}$"

6"

$49\frac{1}{2}$"

$\frac{7}{8}$"

$\frac{3}{4}$"

1"

$1\frac{1}{2}$"

$1\frac{1}{4}$"

$\frac{1}{2}$"

$\frac{7}{16}$"

16"

15"

63

ROCKING CHAIR

PRIVATE COLLECTION

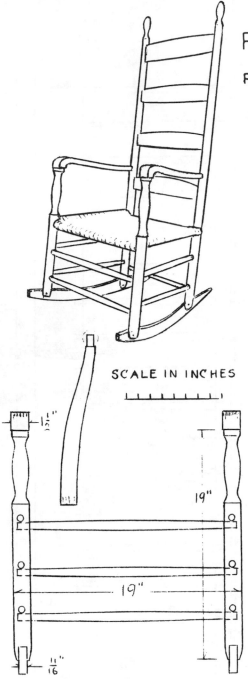

SCALE IN INCHES

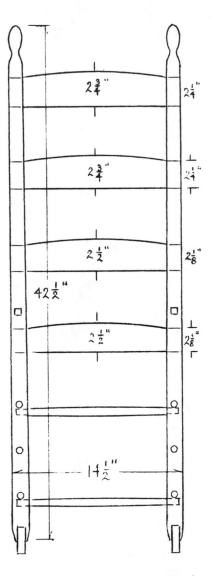

$2\frac{3}{4}$"

$2\frac{1}{4}$"

$2\frac{3}{4}$"

$2\frac{1}{4}$"

$2\frac{1}{2}$"

$2\frac{1}{8}$"

$42\frac{1}{2}$"

$2\frac{1}{2}$"

$2\frac{1}{8}$"

$1\frac{1}{2}$"

19"

$14\frac{1}{2}$"

19"

$\frac{11}{16}$"

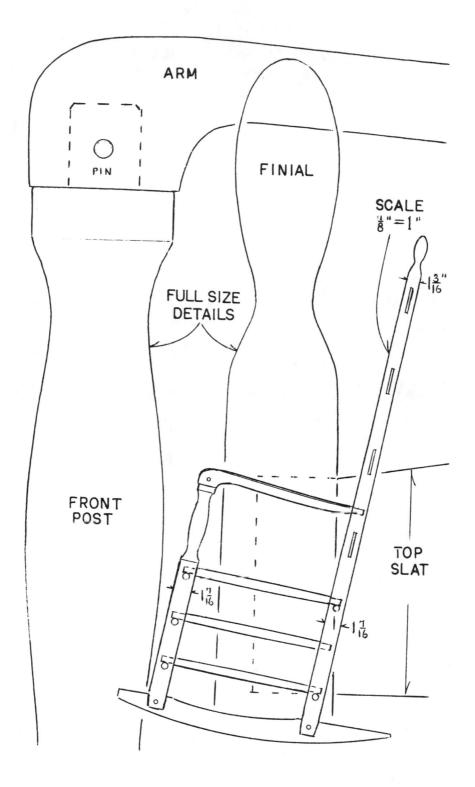

ARM

PIN

FINIAL

SCALE
$\frac{1}{8}" = 1"$

$1\frac{3}{16}"$

FULL SIZE
DETAILS

FRONT
POST

TOP
SLAT

$1\frac{7}{16}$

$1\frac{7}{16}$

FOOTSTOOL
HANCOCK SHAKER VILLAGE,
HANCOCK MASS.

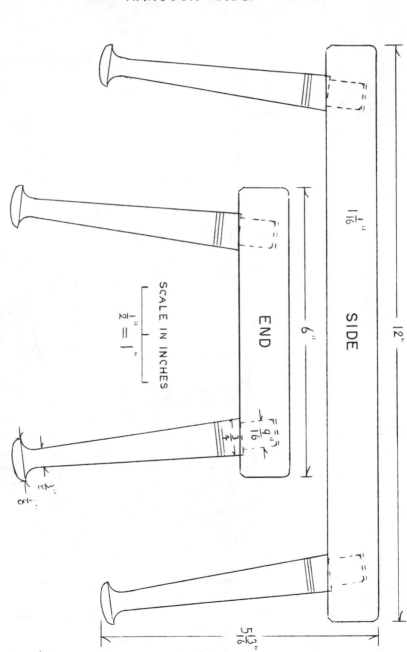

SCALE IN INCHES

$\frac{1}{2}" = 1"$

END

SIDE

$1\frac{1}{16}"$

$6"$

$12"$

$\frac{9}{16}"$

$\frac{3}{4}"$

$5\frac{13}{16}"$

FOOTSTOOL
HANCOCK SHAKER VILLAGE, HANCOCK MASS.

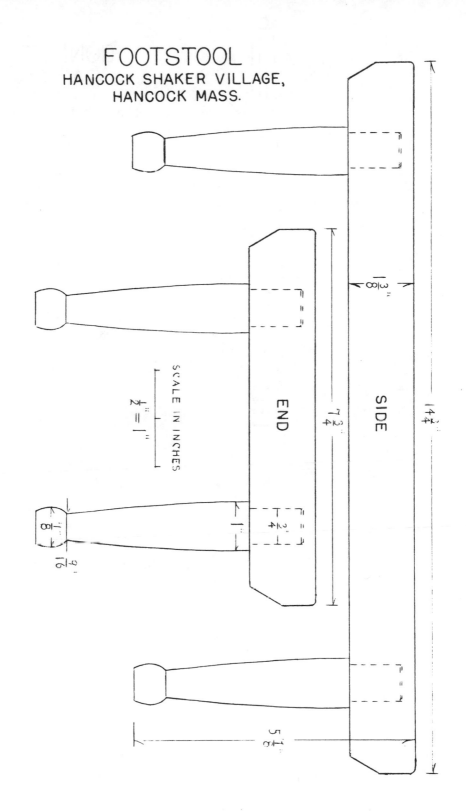

SCALE IN INCHES
$\frac{1}{2}" = 1"$

END

SIDE

$1\frac{3}{8}"$

$7\frac{2}{4}"$

$14\frac{2}{4}"$

$2\frac{3}{4}"$

$1"$

$1"$

$1\frac{1}{8}"$

$\frac{9}{16}"$

$5\frac{1}{8}"$

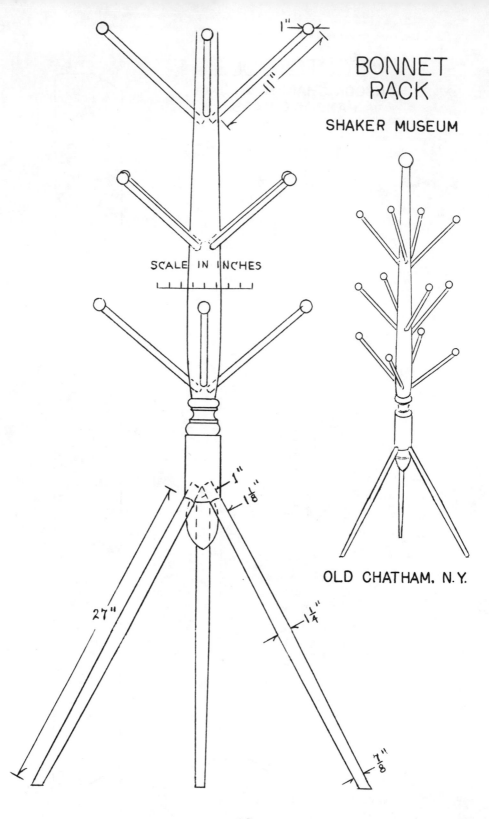

BONNET
RACK

SHAKER MUSEUM

1"

11"

SCALE IN INCHES

1"

1⅛"

OLD CHATHAM, N.Y.

27"

1¼"

⅞"

68

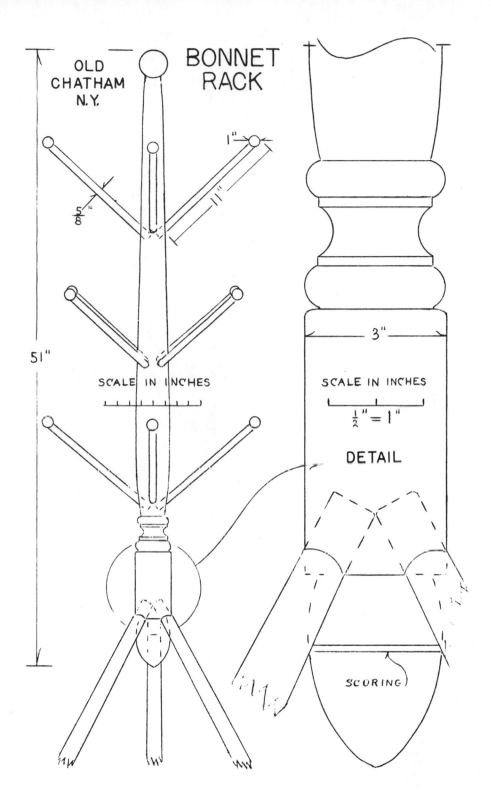

OLD CHATHAM N.Y.

BONNET RACK

51"

1"

1"

5/8"

SCALE IN INCHES

3"

SCALE IN INCHES

1/2" = 1"

DETAIL

SCORING

69

LANTERN
THE CHATHAM MUSEUM, OLD CHATHAM, N.Y.

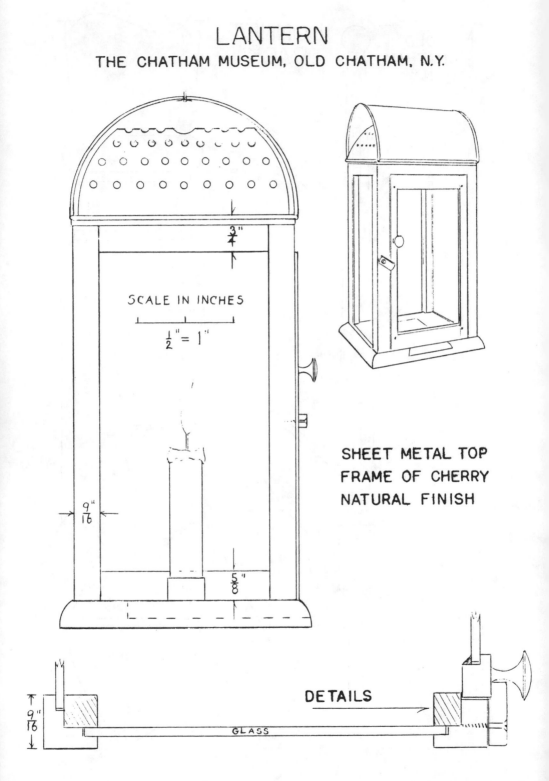

SCALE IN INCHES

$\frac{1}{2}" = 1"$

$\frac{3}{4}"$

$\frac{9}{16}"$

$\frac{5}{8}"$

SHEET METAL TOP
FRAME OF CHERRY
NATURAL FINISH

DETAILS

GLASS

$\frac{9}{16}"$

LANTERN

THE CHATHAM MUSEUM, OLD CHATHAM, N.Y.

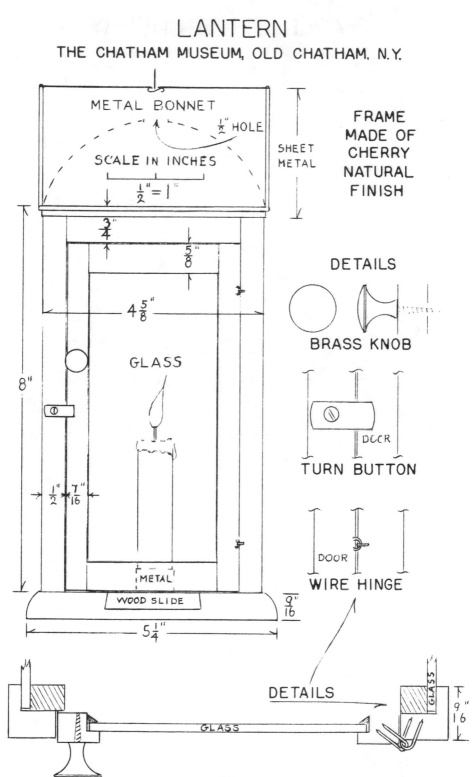

METAL BONNET

$\frac{1}{2}$" HOLE

SCALE IN INCHES

$\frac{1}{2}$" = 1"

SHEET METAL

FRAME MADE OF CHERRY NATURAL FINISH

$\frac{3}{4}$"

$\frac{5}{8}$"

$4\frac{5}{8}$"

GLASS

8"

$\frac{1}{2}$" $\frac{7}{16}$"

METAL

WOOD SLIDE

$\frac{9}{16}$"

$5\frac{1}{4}$"

DETAILS

BRASS KNOB

TURN BUTTON

DOOR

WIRE HINGE

DOOR

DETAILS

GLASS

GLASS

$\frac{9}{16}$"

MAPLE BIRCH CHERRY

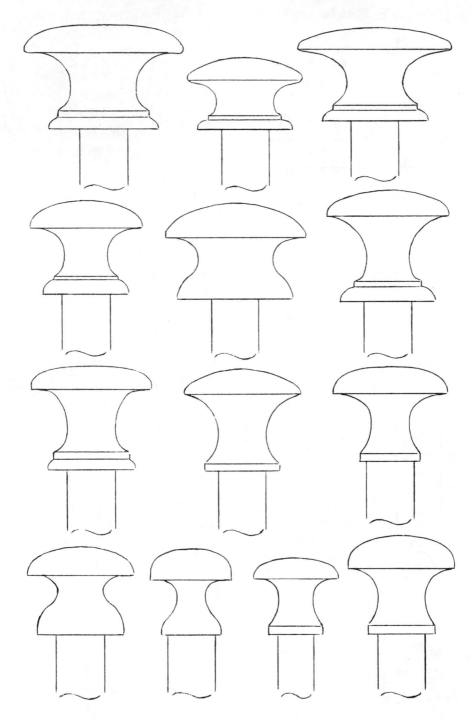

KNOBS AND PULLS

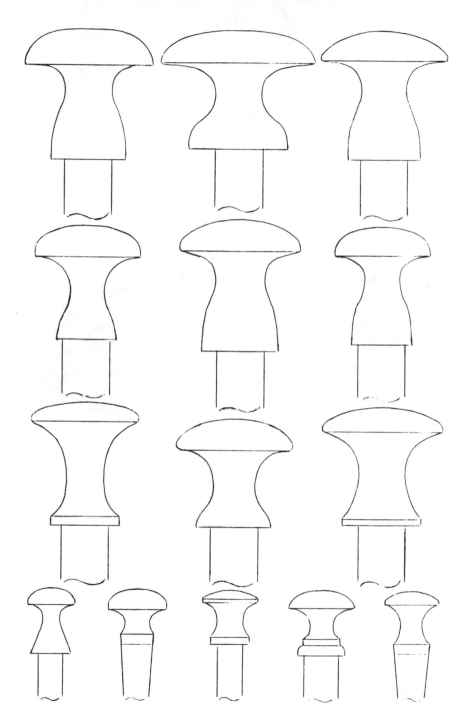

DRESSMAKER'S WEIGHT
MAPLE

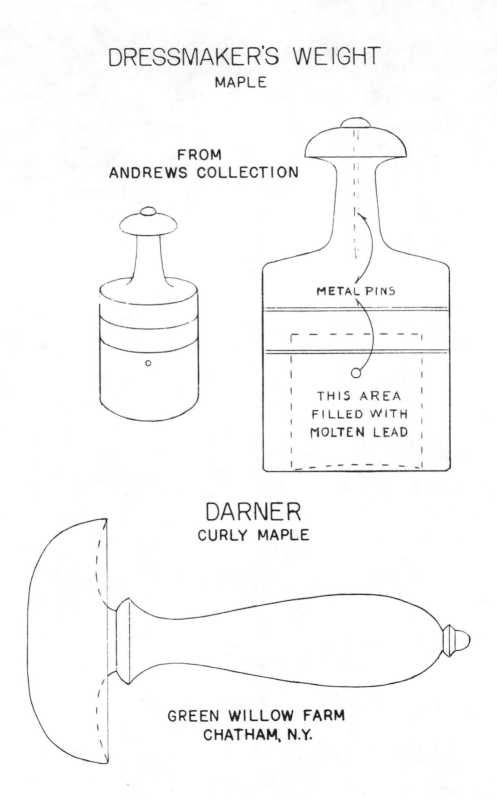

FROM
ANDREWS COLLECTION

METAL PINS

THIS AREA
FILLED WITH
MOLTEN LEAD

DARNER
CURLY MAPLE

GREEN WILLOW FARM
CHATHAM, N.Y.

On the following pages are measured drawings of a secretary or fall-front desk which I made for my own use.

It follows closely the design of two original early pieces of Shaker furniture and therefore must be clearly signed and dated as a Shaker type piece of furniture. Photograph on page 84.

E.H.

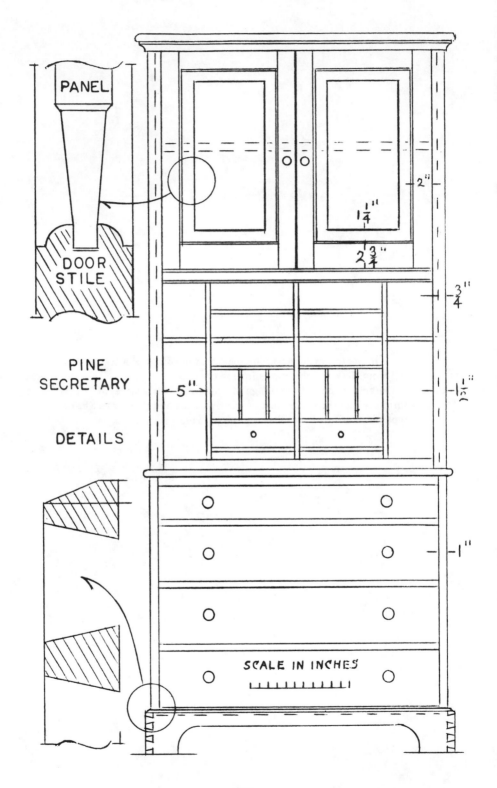

PANEL

DOOR
STILE

PINE
SECRETARY

DETAILS

2"

$1\frac{1}{4}$"

$2\frac{3}{4}$"

$\frac{3}{4}$"

$1\frac{1}{2}$"

5"

1"

SCALE IN INCHES

76

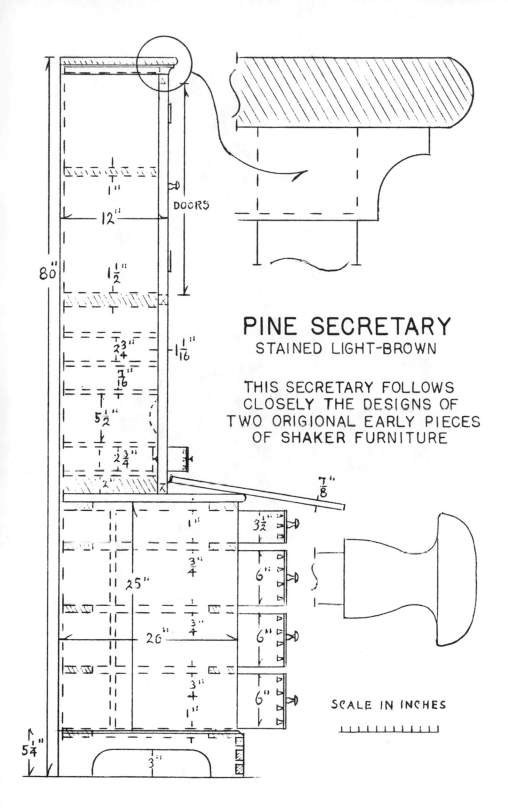

DOORS

80"

12"

1"

1½"

2¾"
7/16"

5½"

2¾"

2"

1 1/16"

PINE SECRETARY
STAINED LIGHT-BROWN

THIS SECRETARY FOLLOWS
CLOSELY THE DESIGNS OF
TWO ORIGIONAL EARLY PIECES
OF SHAKER FURNITURE

7/8"

1"

3/4"

25"

1/2"

3/4"

26"

3/4"

1"

3½"

6"

6"

6"

SCALE IN INCHES

5¼"

3"

High Cupboard Chest—page 8

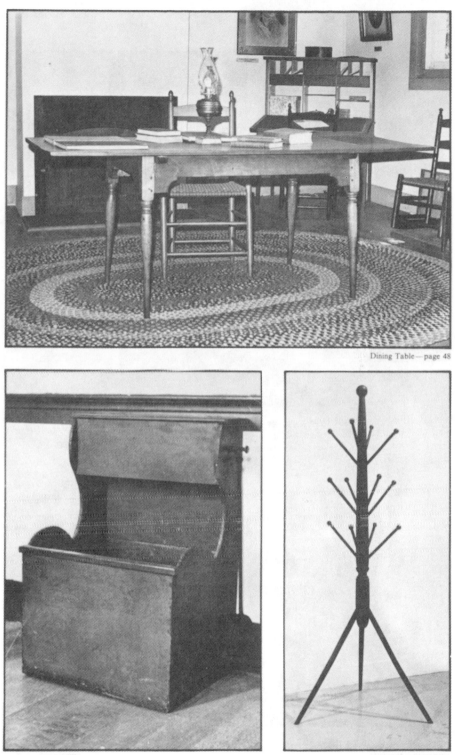

Dining Table—page 48

Wood Box—page 60

Bonnet Rack—page 68

Upright Desk — page 30

Pine Wash Stand—page 46   Case of Drawers—page 28

Storage Bench—page 22

Pie-Safe—page 2

Shaker Type Secretary—page 76

INDEX

BOOKS ON SHAKER FROM BERKSHIRE HOUSE, PUBLISHERS

BY EJNER HANDBERG

Shop Drawings of Shaker Furniture
and Woodenware, Vols. 1, 2, 3

Measured Drawings of Shaker
Furniture and Woodenware

FIELD GUIDES TO SHAKER ANTIQUES

Shaker Woodenware, Vol. 1

Shaker Woodenware, Vol. 2 (Spring 1992)

Shaker Baskets and Poplarware
(Spring 1992)

Shaker Textiles, Costume and Fancy
Goods (Forthcoming)

Shaker Paper (Forthcoming)

Shaker Iron, Tin, and Brass
(Forthcoming)

Shaker Furniture (Forthcoming)

OTHER BOOKS FROM BERKSHIRE HOUSE

TRAVEL: THE GREAT DESTINATIONS SERIES

The Berkshire Book: A Complete Guide

The Santa Fe and Taos Book

The Napa and Sonoma Book

The Chesapeake Bay Book (Spring 1992)

The Coast of Maine Book (Spring 1992)

RECREATION

Music Festivals in America

Yukon Wild

BERKSHIRE OUTDOORS SERIES

Hikes & Walks in the Berkshire Hills

Skiing in the Berkshire Hills

Bike Rides in the Berkshire Hills